Utah

UTAH BY ROAD

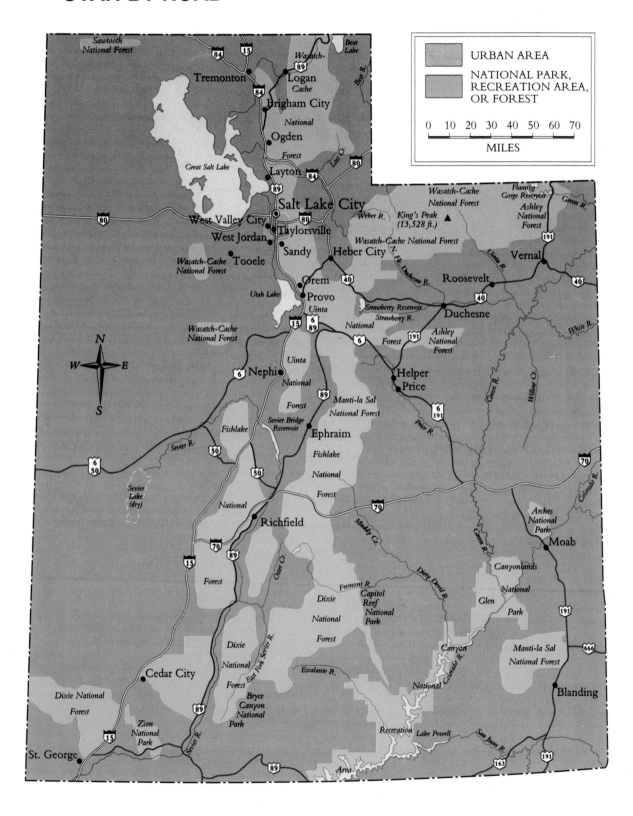

URBAN AREA

NATIONAL PARK,
RECREATION AREA,
OR FOREST

0 10 20 30 40 50 60 70
MILES

Sawtooth
National Forest

Bear
Lake

Wasatch-

Tremonton

Logan
Cache

Brigham City

National

Ogden

Forest

Layton

Great Salt Lake

Salt Lake City

West Valley City

Weber R.

Wasatch-Cache
National Forest

King's Peak
(13,528 ft.)

Flaming
Gorge Reservoir

Green R.

Ashley
National
Forest

Taylorsville

West Jordan

Wasatch-Cache National Forest

Uinta R.

Vernal

Sandy

Heber City

Wasatch-Cache
National Forest

Tooele

Orem

Provo

Roosevelt

Duchesne

Utah Lake

Uinta

Strawberry Reservoir

Strawberry R.

Ashley
National
Forest

White R.

Wasatch-Cache
National Forest

National

Forest

Sevier R.

Nephi

Uinta

National

Forest

Sevier Bridge
Reservoir

Manti-la Sal
National Forest

Helper
Price

Price R.

Ephraim

Fishlake

Fishlake

National

Forest

Muddy Cr.

Green R.

Willow Cr.

Sevier Lake
(dry)

National

Richfield

Otter Cr.

Dirty Devil R.

Arches
National
Park

Canyonlands

Moab

Colorado R.

Forest

Fremont R.

Capitol
Reef
National
Park

National

Glen

Park

Manti-la Sal
National Forest

Dixie

Dixie

National

Forest

East Fork Sevier R.

Escalante R.

Canyon

Colorado R.

National

Cedar City

Dixie National

Forest

Bryce
Canyon
National
Park

Recreation

Lake Powell

Blanding

Zion
National
Park

Sevier R.

St. George

Area

San Juan R.

Celebrate the States

Utah

Rebecca Stefoff and Wendy Mead

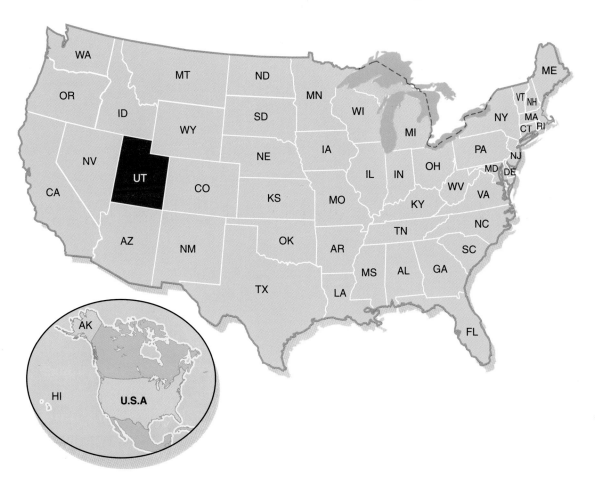

Marshall Cavendish
Benchmark

New York

Marshall Cavendish Benchmark
99 White Plains Road
Tarrytown, NY 10591-5502
www.marshallcavendish.us

Library of Congress Cataloging-in-Publication Data
Stefoff, Rebecca, 1951–
Utah / by Rebecca Stefoff and Wendy Mead.—2nd ed.
p. cm. — (Celebrate the states)
Summary: "Provides comprehensive information on the geography, history, wildlife, governmental
structure, economy, cultural diversity, peoples, religion, and landmarks of
Utah"—Provided by publisher.
Includes bibliographical references and index.
ISBN 978-0-7614-4035-2
1. Utah—Juvenile literature. I. Mead, Wendy. II. Title.

F826.3.S743 2009
979.2—dc22
2008040026

Editor: Christine Florie
Co-Editor: Denise Pangia
Publisher: Michelle Bisson
Art Director: Anahid Hamparian
Series Designer: Adam Mietlowski

Photo research and layout by Marshall Cavendish International (Asia) Private Limited—
Thomas Khoo, Benson Tan and Shawn Wee

Cover photo by Corbis

The photographs in this book are used by permission and through the courtesy of, *Photolibrary*:
back cover, 8, 10, 14, 15, 17, 19, 20, 21, 24, 29, 31, 33, 39, 60, 62, 64, 65, 66, 68, 77, 80, 82,
87, 88, 90, 96, 97, 99, 105, 106, 109, 113, 117, 130, 131, 132, 134, 135; *Getty Images*: 12, 23,
34, 47, 50, 52, 55, 85, 121, 123, 125, 126, 128; *Photolibrary / Alamy*: 26, 35, 44, 58, 118, 120,
129, 133, 137; *Corbis*: 36, 38, 43, 74, 94, 102, 122; *Reuters*: 48; *AP Photo / Douglas C Pizac*: 72.

Printed in Malaysia
1 3 5 6 4 2

Contents

Utah Is . . .

Utah is an awe-inspiring landscape.

"There are deep caverns and rooms resembling ruins of prisons, castles, churches with their guarded walls, battlements, spires, and steeples, niches and recesses, presenting the wildest and most wonderful scene that the eye of man ever beheld; in fact, it is one of the wonders of the world."
> —government surveyor T. C. Bailey, describing Bryce Canyon, 1876

Utah was founded as a religious colony by the Mormons, who have had a strong influence on the state.

"There is much else about our state's past that is exciting and instructive, but we cannot escape the importance of the Mormon presence or influence here."
> —historian Dean L. May

Yet what was once meant to be a religious state has evolved into a more diverse place.

"It will not be the same experience growing up in Utah now as it was fifty, forty, or even thirty years ago. It never will be again. The genie is out of the bottle, because we are connecting more globally. I call it the new Utah."
> —Pam Perlich, research economist at the University of Utah

"Utah's becoming more and more diverse. That adds to the quality of life and attracts all sorts of migration."
> —Juliette Tennert, chief economist and demographer, Governor's Office of Planning and Budget

As the state's population continues to increase, Utah faces daunting challenges.

"We must not leave our grandchildren a legacy of crowded parks and recreation areas, a shortage of farmland and urban open spaces, and a loss of native wildlife. We must not be too shortsighted to make the basic commitment to protect our own natural assets."

—Lewis K. Billings, mayor of Provo

"Along with the benefits, Utah is encountering all the problems of growth: school overcrowding, heavy traffic, and loss of green space and the agricultural occupations. . . . [Utahns'] natural tendency to welcome new residents and jobs has been tempered by the fear of seeing their mountain paradise become increasingly urban."

—author Cynthia Larsen Bennett

Utahns are up for the tasks ahead, making their state one of the most prosperous and inviting places in the nation.

"Now is the time to be hopeful and visionary, to appreciate our exciting place in history, to lead out, and—by so doing—to capture the abundant promises of Utah's tomorrow."

—Governor Jon M. Huntsman Jr.

From snowcapped peaks in the north to red-rock canyons and windswept deserts in the south, Utah is ruggedly beautiful. American Indians dwelt in this stern, dry, rocky land for thousands of years before waves of newcomers arrived, each seeking something. Mormons wanted a religious homeland, prospectors wanted riches, Hispanic, Greeks, Italians, Japanese, and other immigrants wanted a chance at a better life. People still visit Utah: mountain bikers searching for thrilling new trails, snowboarders and skiers enjoying the snow, families looking for happiness in an orderly suburb or a quiet country town. Sometimes called "the land no one wanted," Utah turns out to have exactly what many have sought.

Chapter One

A Land of Extremes

More and more people are calling Utah home, drawn in part by the state's breathtaking beauty. This western state has nearly every type of landform or body of water imaginable. Towering mountains, lush forests and valleys, winding rivers, serene lakes, and stunning red-rock cliffs are all found here. With all of these environmental wonders, the state must wrestle with increased demand for land and natural resources while protecting its amazing geological features and unusual landscapes.

Geologist Clarence Dutton felt the magic and majesty of this land. In 1880, after visiting Zion Canyon in southwestern Utah, he wrote of its massive rock walls: "There is an eloquence to their forms which stirs the imagination with a singular power. . . . Nothing can exceed the wondrous beauty of Zion . . . in the nobility and beauty of the sculptures there is no comparison." Many others have felt the same sense of awe. Utah seems much larger than life. The state's mountains are massive and impressive—Paula Huff, author of *Hiking Utah's Summits*, calls Utah "the rooftop of the United States." Utah's gorges and valleys are nearly as deep and every bit as grand as the Grand Canyon, which lies just across the

Utah's landscape is varied, ranging from brilliant red-rock cliffs to quiet green valleys.

Zion Canyon, part of Zion National Park, is located in the Colorado Plateau Province.

border in Arizona. The state also contains the nation's biggest lake west of the Mississippi River—the Great Salt Lake—and two of the country's major rivers.

Utah sits on the western slope of the Rocky Mountains, the backbone of the American West. It is bordered by Colorado on the east, Arizona on the south, Nevada on the west, Idaho on the north, and Wyoming on the northeast. Utah is divided among three dramatically different geographic areas. They are the Rocky Mountain System, Basin and Range, and Colorado Plateau provinces.

LAND AND WATER

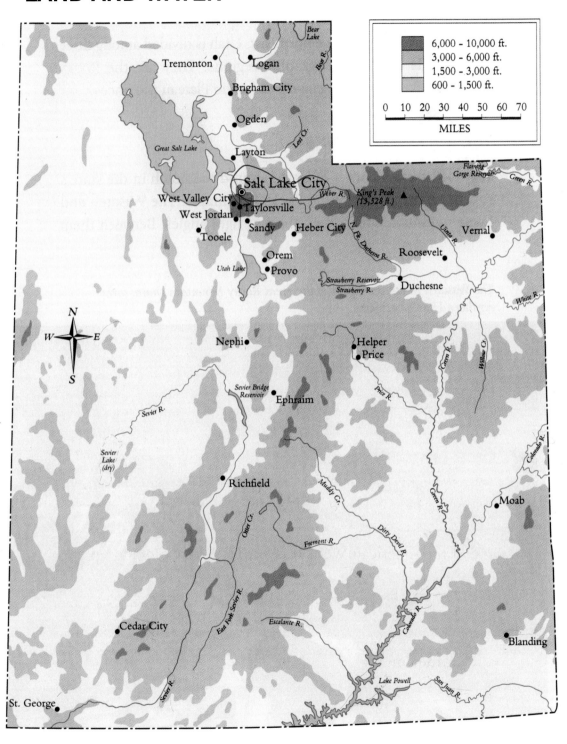

Legend:
- 6,000 – 10,000 ft.
- 3,000 – 6,000 ft.
- 1,500 – 3,000 ft.
- 600 – 1,500 ft.

0 10 20 30 40 50 60 70
MILES

Bear Lake

Tremonton
Logan
Brigham City
Bear R.
Ogden
Lost Cr.
Great Salt Lake
Layton
Salt Lake City
West Valley City
Taylorsville
West Jordan
Sandy
Tooele
Heber City
Orem
Utah Lake
Provo
Weber R.
Flaming Gorge Reservoir
Green R.
King's Peak (13,528 ft.)
Ft. Duchesne R.
Uinta R.
Vernal
Roosevelt
Strawberry Reservoir
Strawberry R.
Duchesne
White R.

N
W   E
S

Nephi
Helper
Price
Green R.
Willow Cr.
Sevier Bridge Reservoir
Ephraim
Price R.
Sevier R.
Sevier Lake (dry)
Richfield
Muddy Cr.
Colorado R.
Moab
Otter Cr.
Fremont R.
Dirty Devil R.
Green R.
Cedar City
East Fork Sevier R.
Escalante R.
Colorado R.
Blanding
Sevier R.
Lake Powell
San Juan R.
St. George

THE ROCKY MOUNTAINS

The northeastern corner of Utah, around the notch in the state's square border, is part of the Rocky Mountains. The Wasatch and Uinta mountain ranges meet there at right angles. Between them are green, well-watered valleys. The Cache Valley, a patchwork of tidy farms, orchards, and pastures, is the most fertile part of Utah.

The Green River is the biggest waterway in the region. It flows south from Wyoming into Utah. In 1963 construction crews completed a dam on the river, creating a long lake known as the Flaming Gorge Reservoir. This reservoir is the centerpiece of the Flaming Gorge National Recreation Area, which Utah shares with Wyoming. After passing the dam, the Green River curves briefly into Colorado before it winds and twists its way south into the hilly heart of Utah.

Utah's highest mountains are in the Rocky Mountain Province. Many of the Uinta Mountains' rounded peaks are around 13,000 feet

The Wasatch Mountains divides the Rocky Mountain and Basin and Range provinces.

(3,962 meters) high. Utah's highest point, Kings Peak, rises above the rest of the Uintas to a height of 13,528 feet (4,123 m). The Wasatch Mountains stretch south from the Idaho border to Central Utah. The eastern side of the Wasatch Range rises gently from valleys to jagged, snowy summits. On its western edge, however, the mountain wall is steep and sheer. It forms a rugged line of cliffs and slopes called the Wasatch Front, which drops abruptly from the peaks to the flatland 7,000 feet (2,134 m) below. There the Basin and Range Province begins.

BASIN AND RANGE

The Basin and Range Province, which covers all of western Utah and continues into Nevada, consists of many low, blunt-topped, north-south mountain ranges that one early explorer described as "an army of caterpillars marching to Mexico." The ranges are separated by flat, level valleys called basins.

The Basin and Range Province contains some of the least hospitable landscapes in the United States. Words of the old folk song "Sweet Betsy from Pike," which told of the journey of gold hunters to California in the late 1840s, probably refer to those landscapes: "They came to the desert and salt water lakes / The ground it was teemin' with varmints and snakes."

This part of Utah certainly has deserts, notably the Great Salt Lake Desert in the northwest, the Sevier Desert in the central west, and the Escalante Desert in the southwest. The Sevier and Escalante deserts are dry, treeless flatlands similar to many other regions in the West. The Great Salt Lake Desert, however, is unique. Glaringly white and as shiny as glass, it is covered with a thick crust of salt laid down long ago when the ancient

When early visitors tried to cross the Great Salt Lake Desert, they were surprised to find mud lying beneath its hard, salty surface.

sea that once covered the land eventually dried up. American Indians and early explorers feared crossing this waterless wasteland.

One of Utah's most famous bodies of water is the Great Salt Lake, which gets its salt from minerals in the soil. This huge, shallow lake has no outlets. Water that enters the lake stays there, which means that the lake—which averages more than 1 million acres (404,686 hectares) in area—gets larger or smaller depending upon seasonal rainfall and snowmelt.

In a wet year the lake's average depth can increase from about 13 to 14 feet (4 to 4.3 m) to more than 35 feet (11 m). An especially heavy snowfall can cause the lake's waters to spill over its banks to cover freeways, farms, industrial sites, and even Salt Lake City's international airport. In a dry year the lake is shallow and saltier than ever because there is little freshwater to dilute the minerals. At such times the Great Salt Lake reveals its most astounding feature: you can float in it with remarkable ease, because objects, including swimmers, float higher in saltwater than in fresh. If you take a dip in the Great Salt Lake when it is low and extra salty, you will find it almost impossible to swim underwater!

THE COLORADO PLATEAU

Most of eastern and southern Utah—more than half of the state—is part of the Colorado Plateau, which covers the Four Corners region where Colorado, New Mexico, Arizona, and Utah meet. The Colorado Plateau is a broad, rocky highland, but it is not a smooth and flat tableland as its name suggests. In some places, layers of rock that lie under the region tilt upward. Their edges are worn away to expose three enormous rows of cliffs, stacked on top of one another. Because each layer is a different color, these are called the Pink, White, and Vermilion (red) Cliffs. Together they create an immense landform called the Grand Staircase of Utah. Elsewhere in the Colorado Plateau are mountains and uncountable ridges, folds,

Worn away over time, the Vermilion Cliffs tell of the story of Utah's geological past.

hills, saw-toothed rock reefs, hoodoos (tall spires of rock), mesas (flat-topped, steep-sided uplands), and buttes (similar to mesas but smaller). At 10,388 feet (3,170 m) high, Navajo Mountain near the Arizona border is far from the tallest mountain in Utah's Colorado Plateau Province, but its broad, cone-shaped profile dominates the horizon for miles around.

These towering features of the landscape are intermingled with gorges, canyons, and valleys that plunge to depths far below the level of the plateau. The Green and Colorado rivers, which meet in southeastern Utah, carved the widest and deepest of these canyons over millions of years. The Glen Canyon Dam, located just over the Utah border in Arizona, backs the waters of the Colorado up into miles and miles of branching canyons to form Lake Powell, Utah's largest human-made lake.

Fertile valleys nestle among the High Plateau Mountains at the region's western edge, and forests carpet some mountaintops and uplands, but much of the Colorado Plateau is desert. The earth surface is worn and windswept rock with only a few pockets of soil here and there to offer a roothold to hardy plants.

WILD UTAH

In the 1950s writer Edward Abbey worked as a ranger in what is now Arches National Park in southeastern Utah. His 1968 book about the experience, *Desert Solitaire: A Season in the Wilderness*, captured the extraordinary beauty of a landscape unknown to most people: "The desert waits outside, desolate and still and strange, unfamiliar and often grotesque in its forms and colors, inhabited by rare, furtive creatures

Lake Powell is one of the largest reservoirs in North America.

of incredible hardiness and cunning, sparingly colonized by weird mutants from the plant kingdom, most of them as spiny, thorny, stunted and twisted as they are tenacious."

The plants of the desert and canyons include aromatic sagebrush shrubs and tough mountain juniper trees. (Early settlers wrongly called the mountain junipers cedars, which is why many place-names in Utah include the word cedar.) Willow and cottonwood trees grow along the courses of rivers and streams, forming narrow corridors of green across the land. Spruce and fir flourish in the cooler, moister districts. Aspens, whose delicate leaves turn bright gold in the fall, line alpine clearings and meadows. Rarest and most impressive of trees is the bristlecone pine, which grows only in high, windy, open places like cliff tops and mountain ledges. Bristlecones are among the longest-lived species on Earth; some of these ancient trees in Utah are more than three thousand years old. They are not towering forest giants, though—their trunks are gnarled and twisted, and they grow low and close to the ground.

For a short time each year, even the most barren tracts of Utah blaze forth in a glory of wildflowers. Purple-blue lupine and red Indian paintbrush nod in the breeze along country roads. Utah's state flower, the sego lily, carpets meadows with white, lilac, or yellow blossoms. Crevices among desert rocks glow with the greenish white flowers of yucca plants, raised high on stiff stalks, and with the white, salmon pink, orange, and red blooms of the prickly pear cactus, delicate petals set amid menacing spikes.

From mountain lakes to desert canyons, Utah's habitats are home to a great number of animal species. The Great Salt Lake, Utah Lake (south of the salt lake), and Bear Lake (straddling the Idaho border) provide habitat for hundreds of thousands of seagulls and other waterbirds. Some of these

Utah is home to many unusual plants and trees, such as this bristlecone pine.

birds live in Utah year-round, while others rest and feed there during migration. They eat many of the tiny brine shrimp that live in the Great Salt Lake and the brine flies that haunt the lake's shores. Other bodies of water in the state have such fish as trout, catfish, carp, and bass.

Black bears live in the mountains, but they are not really black—in Utah they tend to be golden brown to match the earth tones of the landscape. Rocky Mountain sheep, mountain goats, and mountain lions dwell, as you might expect, in the mountains. So do bobcats and beavers. Coyotes live throughout the state. Elk graze in mountain meadows, pronghorn antelope on plateau grasslands, and mule deer along canyon streams. Although some large animals such as mountain lions live in the arid canyons, most of the wildlife there is small: mice, snakes, slow-moving tortoises, and lizards. Desert hikers soon learn to check their boots and bedrolls for scorpions— flat, fast-moving creatures whose stingers pack a poisonous punch.

While scorpions may be plentiful in the state, Utah is also home to eighteen of the nation's endangered and threatened species. An endangered mollusk, the Kanab ambersnail, can be found only in a very small area of the south-central part of the state. Two of the

Pronghorn antelope like to feed on grasses, sagebrush, and other plants.

state's endangered birds—the Mexican spotted owl and the southwestern willow flycatcher— reside mostly in the south.

The Mexican spotted owl is facing extinction.

One threatened species, the Utah prairie dog, lives in the southwestern and south-central parts of the state. Prairie dogs—there are three different species found in Utah—have been considered pests, especially by farmers and ranchers. Over the years there have been widespread efforts to eradicate them, including a poisoning campaign during the 1950s. Those tactics seriously diminished the Utah prairie dog population, earning the small animal a place on the federal endangered species list in 1973. There was some growth in the size of the animal's population, however, so its listing was upgraded to threatened in 1984. The species has a long way yet to go before it has fully recovered. It still has to overcome habitat loss, disease, and human intervention.

In addition to endangered wildlife, a number of the state's plants are facing extinction. Twenty-four plant species are listed as either endangered or threatened, including the autumn buttercup. Found only in the Sevier River valley, this bright yellow wildflower has been seen by a lucky few. Efforts are also underway to see if this endangered plant can be grown elsewhere and reintroduced into the Utah wilderness.

Scientists are working to save the autumn buttercup.

SUN, RAIN, AND SNOW

After her first visit to Utah, Oregonian Kathy Carilla offered this advice to anyone planning a similar trip: "Bring extra sunblock!" Sun worshipers love Utah—the state gets an average of 237 sunny days per year. Temperatures vary widely, though, and the mountains and high valleys are considerably cooler than the deserts and southern canyons. Utah's highest recorded temperature was 117 degrees Fahrenheit (47 degrees Celsius) in the southern city of Saint George in 1985. Its lowest was –69 °F (–56 °C) at Peter's Sink that same year. Winters are rarely severe except in the high mountains, while summers are long, hot, and dry. Nonetheless, in the worst hot spells people can cool off by going up the nearest mountain.

Like temperature, precipitation—the total amount of rain and snow—varies dramatically across the state. The driest region, the Great Salt Lake Desert, gets less than 5 inches (13 centimeters) of precipitation a year. The wettest region, the Wasatch Range, receives about 40 inches (102 cm), enough to provide plenty of snow for skiers at Alta, Park City, and other mountain ski resorts.

In summer, thunderstorms frequently stir the skies over the Colorado Plateau. Edward Abbey described the skies of August in southern Utah: "By noon the clouds are forming around the horizon and in the afternoon, predictable as sunrise and sunset, they gather in massed formations, colliding in jags of lightning and thunderous artillery, and pile higher and higher toward the summit of the sky in vaporish mountains, dazzling under the sunlight." Often, however, no rain falls from these impressive displays. Or it falls but evaporates in the hot air before reaching the ground. Weather scientists call this phenomenon virga. It is a common sight over the plateau: a veil of rain, dark against the sky, that doesn't touch the earth.

This image captures a virga, or a storm with no rain or precipitation, that touches the ground.

IMPROVING AIR QUALITY

With new residents arriving every day, Utah is working to address some of the pollution problems that sometimes accompany extensive growth. Car exhaust and emissions from power plants are some of the contributing factors in air pollution.

The American Lung Association (ALA) has studied air quality around the country and made some disturbing findings in Utah. Cache, Salt Lake, and Utah counties all made the list for the twenty-five counties in the United States most polluted by short-term particle pollution in the ALA's *State of the Air 2008* report. Particle pollution comes from ash,

The state government is looking for ways to cut down its dependence on coal-burning power plants for energy.

soot, chemicals, exhaust fumes, and other materials. These particles get mixed into the air and can cause a variety of health problems, including heart disease and lung cancer. It also makes breathing more difficult for people who have asthma or other respiratory diseases.

Utah also battles ozone pollution—sometimes called smog. When the vapors from cars, factories, trucks, and power plants react with sunlight, ozone gas is formed. Breathing in this gas can irritate a person's respiratory system. It is especially dangerous for senior citizens, children, and those individuals who already have breathing problems. To protect the public the Utah Department of Environmental Quality provides residents with daily reports on the condition of the air and issues warnings when the air quality is bad.

Two of the state's most populated areas, Davis and Salt Lake counties, had the most high ozone days from 2004 to 2006, according to the ALA publication. While the Wasatch Front region may have the worst pollution, it is not uncommon to see smog in other parts of the state as well, even at its famous recreational areas such as Zion National Park.

To combat this problem the state is exploring other energy sources, such as geothermal energy, solar energy, and wind power. Using these resources to produce electricity will reduce Utah's dependence on coal-fueled plants, which themselves create more harmful emissions. Some local governments, such as the city of Moab, are also looking at using more environmentally friendly vehicles, such as electric cars.

Chapter Two

"This Is the Right Place"

The story of Utah began millions of years ago, and some traces of its ancient past can be found on the state's eastern border. At Dinosaur National Monument scientists have found evidence of the life that stomped through Utah's swamps and swam in its seas a hundred million years ago. The tale of human history, however, did not start until much, much later. Between 10,000 and 12,000 years ago the first native peoples lived on this challenging, sometimes unforgiving, land.

AMERICAN-INDIAN CULTURES

The first people in Utah were the Paleo-Indians. They were descended from migrants who entered North America across a land bridge that connected Alaska to Siberia in northeast Asia until about 11,000 years ago. The Paleo-Indians gathered wild plants and hunted birds, rabbits, and other small game.

Brigham Young (center) led an expedition of Mormon pioneers to Utah in 1847.

Evolving into what is known as the Desert Archaic Culture around four thousand years later, they lived in small nomadic groups, traveling around depending on the weather. They learned to make baskets, tools, and other items out of stone, wood, and bone. Only a few of these handmade objects, such as sharp, beautifully carved spear points, have survived to help shed light on the lives of these vanished ancient peoples.

People in this region learned about farming around 500 C.E. The Ancestral Puebloan culture—also sometimes called the Anasazi—moved into southeastern Utah around 400 C.E. They raised corn, beans, squash, cotton, and turkeys. They created dramatic black-and-white pottery and built complex, stable homes of poles, cut stone, and adobe (sun-dried mud brick). After 1150 C.E. they began building large, many-roomed dwellings called pueblos, some perched high on canyon or cliff walls. The center of their civilization, however, lay outside Utah's present borders.

Another mysterious early people were the Fremont, who lived mostly in the western Colorado Plateau and eastern Great Basin regions. Fremont people hunted with bows and arrows, grew corn and vegetables, and made clay pottery and statues. They built sturdy stone or adobe buildings called granaries to store food. Some of these granaries still stand, tucked under rock overhangs or into niches in canyons. The Fremont also carved and painted haunting images of animals, geometric shapes, and broad-shouldered, horned human figures on rock walls throughout Utah.

Both the Fremont and Ancestral Puebloan cultures were fading away by about 1300. Scientists are not sure why. Perhaps drought had parched their farms or attacks by other American-Indian groups had weakened them. A few hundred years later, when European explorers arrived, other American-Indian peoples were living in Utah.

Known as a peaceful people, the Goshute inhabited Utah's western deserts and were highly successful at living in that harsh land. Small bands made up of groups of families moved from place to place in search of foods such as deer, small game, pine nuts, berries, and crickets. To the south the Paiute Indians grew crops and demonstrated their skills as basket makers. Like the Goshute, they were not interested in warfare and suffered frequent attacks from the Ute. The Ute had a reputation as daring buffalo hunters and fierce raiders. They sometimes took Paiute and Goshute Indians captive during their assaults to sell them to the Spaniards as slaves.

Farther north and west the Shoshones farmed corn and other vegetables, fished, hunted small game, and gathered wild foods. Sometime after 1500 some Navajo moved into southeastern Utah from Arizona and New Mexico. The Navajo kept horses and sheep and were masterful weavers and metalworkers. These were the five American-Indian tribes that Europeans met when they entered Utah.

The buffalo was an important source of food for many American Indians in the region.

TURNED TO STONE: A PAIUTE TALE

In Bryce Canyon in southern Utah, thousands upon thousands of reddish pink stone towers, often topped with white stone, march in rows for miles along the valley floor. Called hoodoos, they are remnants of rock layers that had been eroded by rain and frost. Utah's American Indians believed there was a strange magic to the canyon. The Paiutes have a folktale about how the hoodoos came to be:

Long ago, before there were any Indians, the Legend People lived in Bryce Canyon. There were many kinds of Legend People— birds, animals, and lizards—but they all looked like human beings, and they all painted their faces red and white. Some of the Legend People became bad. They fought among themselves and stole from one another. Instead of making useful things, they destroyed them. Worst of all, they forgot to pay proper respect to the spirits. Their wickedness angered the powerful Coyote. Coyote punished the wicked Legend People by turning them into rocks. You can still see them in Bryce Canyon. Some standing in rows, some sitting down, or some holding onto others—all turned to stone. But each is still wearing the color of paint the Legend People wore on their faces before becoming rocks.

THE ARRIVAL OF EUROPEANS

The European explorers of North America inched their way inland from the coasts. Deep in the center of the western section of the continent, Utah was one of the last places in the present United States that they entered.

The first European known to have entered Utah was Juan Antonio Rivera of Santa Fe, New Mexico, an outpost of the Spanish colony in Mexico. In 1765 he led a party of explorers as far north as present-day Moab. Then, in 1776, Francisco Domínguez and Silvestre Vélez de Escalante left Santa Fe in search of a route to the colony of Monterey on the central California coast. They made it all the way to western Central Utah before winter storms sent them back to Santa Fe.

In the years that followed, Spanish and Mexican traders crisscrossed southern Utah, doing trading and dealing with the American Indians along their route between New Mexico and California. When Mexico became independent in 1821, it claimed Utah as part of its northern territory, but in the 1820s outsiders began entering the region. The English came down from Canada, and Americans came along the Green River. Both sought

one of the West's most valuable resources—the sleek, waterproof hide of the beaver, much prized by hatmakers and coat makers in Europe. Trapping beaver and trading with the Indians for more hides, the mountain men, as they came to be called, nearly made the beaver extinct in the American West. They also explored the region thoroughly and paved the way for those who were to come later.

Jim Bridger was one of the first mountain men to see Great Salt Lake.

Some of the mountain men became famous. Jim Bridger is believed to have been one of the first white people to see the Great Salt Lake (he tasted it and thought it was the Pacific Ocean). Jedediah Strong Smith probably knew more about western geography than anyone alive at the time. Smith was the first non-Indian to cross Utah from north to south and from west to east.

Soon the heyday of the rugged mountain men was nearing an end. In their place, other adventurers began crossing Utah's unusual terrain. Benjamin L. E. Bonneville, on leave from the U.S. Army, explored the area in the mid-1830s while trying to establish a fur trading business. On a mission for the federal government, John C. Frémont traveled throughout the region, even parts of it that belonged to Mexico. Frémont made several journeys into Utah in the 1840s, during which he explored the Great Salt and Utah lakes and crossed the Salt Lake Desert.

Already a few parties of American settlers, among them the fateful Donner-Reed Party, had struggled across that desert, bound for California. Most of the early travelers were not all interested in Utah— it was just an obstacle on their way west. But one band of settlers came to stay and has shaped the state to this day.

THE MORMONS

These pioneers were members of the Church of Jesus Christ of Latter-day Saints, sometimes called Mormons or LDS. Their origins lay in upstate New York, where their leader, Joseph Smith, had published a religious text called the Book of Mormon in 1830. Smith's followers added to Christianity the beliefs that Jesus Christ had appeared in America after his death and that an angel had revealed the Book of Mormon to Smith and inspired him to establish a new church.

Smith and the early elders, as adult male Mormons are called, practiced polygamy, or marriage to more than one wife at the same time. They claimed that their religion not only allowed but encouraged plural marriage. Some Americans, however, were outraged by what they viewed

Mormons received much criticism for marrying more than one wife at a time.

as immoral behavior. As a result, the early Mormons faced hostility and violence. Because of this trouble with non-Mormons, Smith decided that his people should create a new home in the wilderness, outside the United States. In early 1844 he sent elders to examine Oregon and California, to "hunt out a good location where we can . . . build a city in a day, and have a government of our own, get up into the mountains, where the devil cannot dig us out, and live in a healthy climate where we can live as old as we have mind to." Later that same year Smith was killed by an angry mob.

A new leader, Brigham Young, declared that the Mormons would settle near the Great Salt Lake. Soon, Young and more than 140 others were making the long journey across the plains on the Mormon Trail, which paralleled the better-known Oregon Trail. Turning south in Wyoming, the pioneers crossed the Wasatch Mountains in midsummer heat and then worked their way to the Great Salt Lake valley. There, in July 1847, at the mouth of Emigration Canyon, Mormon legend claims that Brigham Young took one look around and announced, "This is the right place." In reality, though, Young was ill and was riding in the back of a wagon. Some elders reached the site of Salt Lake City first, dedicated it as the

Mormons' new home, and started plowing. Young's wagon showed up two days later.

Soon thousands of Mormons were traveling the Mormon Trail. By 1860 more than 23,000 Mormons lived in Salt Lake, Davis, Summit, Tooele, and Utah counties. And new believers kept coming. Today's Mormons look back with special pride on the phase of settlement called the Handcart Migration. Between 1856 and 1860 some

Most of the Mormon handcart pioneers started their trek to Utah in either Iowa or Nebraska.

three thousand people walked the Mormon Trail without wagons or draft animals. Instead they hauled their possessions westward for 1,000 miles (1,609 kilometers) in hand-drawn wooden carts. Upon their arrival in Mormon territory, they found neat homes, wide streets, and a temple under construction in Salt Lake City. They also heard the story of how, in 1848, huge swarms of insects had threatened to destroy crops until seagulls from the lake devoured them. The Mormons regarded the gulls as divine intervention, and the California gull is Utah's state bird today.

The Wasatch Front was not the only area the Mormons settled. Young sent out groups of new arrivals to establish communities in southern Utah and in neighboring Idaho, Colorado, Nevada, and Arizona. The struggles of these small, isolated settlements, sustained only by faith, were epic. Some failed, but many took root and prospered.

CLASHES OVER LAND AND RESOURCES

As they settled in their new promised land, the Mormons encountered some difficulty with the state's native peoples. Brigham Young was known for his moderate policy when dealing with American Indians. At first he tried to develop peaceful relations with them and offered gifts of foods and other items. Joseph Smith had believed that the American Indians were related to the Lamanites, an ancient Middle Eastern people mentioned in the Book of Mormon. In the story of Lamanites, they had fallen out of God's good graces and immigrated to North America. In the face of theft or attacks by American Indians, however, Mormon settlers were not reluctant to respond with force.

Particularly challenging was the Mormons' relationship with the Ute. The Ute tribe's practice of trading captured Paiute Indians for goods was morally offensive to the Mormons, and they sought to discourage the practice. In return the Ute suffered greatly from the loss of their hunting and gathering areas as more settlers moved into their lands.

A gruesome conflict erupted between the two groups in 1853 after a Ute man was killed during a trade dispute with some settlers. The victim was a relative of Walkara, a Ute leader, who called for a white man to be killed to settle the dispute.

After the settlers refused, Walkara and some of his followers took matters into their own hands and did kill a white man. Continuing their assault on the settlers, they attacked several homes and stole cattle and horses. Despite Brigham Young's appeal to seek reconciliation, the situation soon escalated into a series of attacks and counterattacks between the Mormon settlers and the Ute peoples. In 1854 Walkara negotiated a peace treaty with Brigham Young and George A. Smith, another leading member of the Mormon Church, which ended the conflict.

While that situation had been defused, tensions continued to flare up over the years. A Ute leader named Tintic and several others started stealing cattle from settlers, which led to a series of clashes between the two groups—known as the Tintic War—in 1856. One of the underlying reasons behind that conflict was the Ute Indians' struggle to find enough food for their peo-

The American Indians conducted several raids on the white settlers.

ple after being displaced from their lands. Another series of violent clashes between the settlers and American Indians—known as the Black Hawk War—started in 1865 over Mormon cattle that was stolen by some Ute Indians. During an attempt to resolve the food problem, a leader named Black Hawk and his party were offended by how one of the Mormons had treated a member of their delegation. Black Hawk and his men retaliated by killing several Mormons and stealing their cattle.

For several years, Black Hawk continued to lead raids, taking cattle and killing many of the whites. While Black Hawk eventually made his peace with the Mormons in 1867, others continued their raids until an official treaty was signed in 1868. Even then some raids occurred on and off for years, until federal troops arrived in 1872 to handle the situation.

The Ute Indians were not the only native people to have conflicts with the Mormon settlers. The Shoshone also found themselves in the midst of a struggle with Mormon settlers over their lands in the Cache Valley in the 1860s. Some Shoshone fought back, attacking the settlers. In retaliation, the territorial government sent in about two hundred members of California Volunteers under the leadership of Colonel Patrick Edward Connor. On the morning of January 29, 1863, the troops attacked a Shoshone winter camp on the Bear River, killing approximately 250 people, 90 of them women and children. That gory event is now known as the Bear River Massacre.

TOWARD STATEHOOD

In addition to their conflicts with American Indians, the Mormons also had some struggles with the U.S. government. They had hoped their new promised land might be its own independent nation outside of the United States—a hope expressed in many forms, including a Mormon song of the time called "The blood-stained wicked nation / From whence the Saints have fled." But in 1848, following the Mexican-American War, Mexico ceded its northern borderlands, including Utah, to the United States.

Once the territory fell under U.S. control, the Mormons realized that complete independence was not possible, but they still envisioned having an independent state. They wanted Congress to create a state called Deseret, from a word used for "honeybee" in the Book of Mormon. Instead, Congress created the Utah Territory, in 1850. Young was named the territorial governor, but he had to share power with non-Mormon officials sent from Washington, D.C.

Out of all the people traveling on the wagon train, only seventeen children survived the Mountain Meadows Massacre.

Many non-Mormons were fearful and suspicious of Mormon ways. They were concerned not only with polygamy but also with the Mormons' shared ownership of property, their tendency to politically act as a group rather than as individuals (they formed their own political party and joked that they all voted the same way). The church's influence on every aspect of members' lives bewildered outsiders.

One consequence of this mistrust was the Utah War of 1857. Believing that the Mormons were rebelling against U.S. authority and breaking U.S. laws, President James Buchanan sent soldiers to Utah. The Mormons regarded them as an invading army, and a group of tense and frightened Mormons, together with some local American Indians, attacked a wagon train of settlers bound for California, killing an estimated 100 to 150 people in the Mountain Meadows Massacre. Fortunately the assault ended without further disasters, although President Buchanan replaced Young as governor of the Utah Territory. Outside Utah, the press printed sensational stories about polygamous marriages and the church's ruthless treatment of those who defied it. Such stories, some untrue, roused popular opinion against the Mormons.

Growing numbers of non-Mormons were entering Utah. During the 1850s most of them simply stopped briefly while on their way to California, but by the 1860s they were coming to work and stay. Non-Mormon communities sprang up around an army camp established near Salt Lake City in 1862. At about that same time, two events helped open Utah to the outside world. In 1861 the first transcontinental telegraph line ran from California to Nebraska through Salt Lake City.

Eight years later an even bigger milestone was reached when two railway lines, one from the west and one from the east, met at Promontory Summit in northern Utah to form the first railroad all across the United States. A special golden spike joined the two lines. The telegraph line carried this message to the world: "The last rail is laid. The last spike is driven. The Pacific railroad is finished."

On May 10, 1869, a celebration was held to mark the completion of the transcontinental railroad.

ALL ARE TALKING OF UTAH

In 1868 the two sections of the transcontinental railway were rapidly approaching each other. Their projected meeting point was at Promontory Summit, a desolate spot northwest of Ogden, Utah. Many Mormons feared the encroaching hostile world. But Brigham Young, the president of the Mormon Church, said, "I wouldn't give much for a religion which could not withstand the coming of a railroad."

Words attributed to John Davis

Music By Henry C. Work

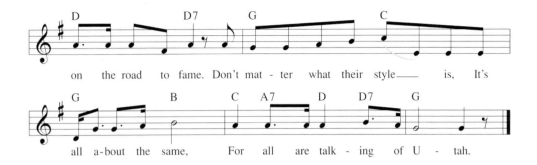

on the road to fame. Don't mat - ter what their style_____ is, It's

all a-bout the same, For all are talk - ing of U - tah.

'Tis Utah and the Mormons in Congress, pulpit, press,
'Tis Utah and the Mormons in every place, I guess.
We must be growing greater, we can't be growing less,
For all are talking of Utah. *Chorus*

They say they'll send an army to set the Mormons right,
Regenerate all Utah, and show us Christian light;
Release our wives and daughters, and put us men to flight,
For all are talking of Utah. *Chorus*

They say that Utah cannot be numbered as a State,
They wished our land divided, but left it rather late.
'Tis hard to tell of Mormons, what yet may be their fate,
For all are talking of Utah. *Chorus*

Whatever may be coming, we cannot well foresee,
For it may be the railroad, or some great prodigy.
At least the noted Mormons are watching what's to be,
For all are talking of Utah. *Chorus*

I now will tell you something you never thought of yet,
We bees are nearly filling the "Hive of Deseret."
If hurt we'll string together, and gather all we get,
For all are talking of Utah. *Chorus*

With the discovery of gold and silver in some Utah mountains in the mid-1860s, prospectors and miners flooded the territory. They hastily built towns of crude wooden buildings high on mountain slopes. To serve them came merchants and traders, many of whom set up shop in Salt Lake City. This growing number of non-Mormons moving to Utah pleased U.S. officials who wanted to "Americanize" the Mormon territory.

Congress firmly refused to consider statehood for Utah until the Mormons gave up polygamy. Congress also passed laws against polygamy that sent hundreds of Mormons to jail and others into hiding. Realizing that Congress would not soften its stand, Wilford Woodruff, the president of the church, in 1890 advised all members "to refrain from contracting any marriage forbidden by the law of the land." The Mormons also disbanded their political party. Recognizing that Utah was moving closer to the mainstream of America, Congress made it the forty-fifth state in 1896.

A YOUNG STATE

Once Utah became a state, its history was linked to that of the United States as a whole. The trends and events that shaped its development were the same ones that swept across the rest of America—the growth of cities, for example. As America slowly shifted from a land of farms to a land of factories, industry replaced agriculture as the state's main source of jobs. By the 1930s less than a fourth of Utahns were farmers.

During the early decades of statehood, Utah's chief industry was mining—not just gold and silver but copper and coal as well. Many people worked in factories related to the mining industry, such as ore smelters and metalworking plants. The rise of the industry brought its own

OUTLAWS

During the late nineteenth and early twentieth centuries the wild terrain of the Colorado Plateau offered hiding places to a number of colorful outlaws. The most famous was Robert LeRoy Parker, who used the name Butch Cassidy (shown on the right). Born in Beaver, Utah, he started out as a cowboy, moved on to cattle stealing, and then became a bank and train robber. During most of the 1890s he led a criminal gang called the Wild Bunch that terro-  rized the West from Montana to Nevada. Between raids they holed up in hideouts such as Robbers' Roost in Utah. Detectives and marshals were closing in on the gang when Cassidy and his partner, Harry Longabaugh, known as the Sundance Kid, fled the area in 1901. They eventually made their way to South America. After an attempt at ranching, they became outlaws there, too, and are believed to have died in a shootout with authorities sometime between 1909 and 1911. But rumors have always shrouded their final moments. Robert Parker's sister later claimed that her brother secretly returned to the United States in 1925 and lived quietly in the Pacific Northwest until his death in 1937.

problems, though. Workers received low wages for long, exhausting work in often dangerous conditions. After an explosion in a coal mine at Winter Quarters, near Scofield, killed two hundred men in 1900, mine workers in Utah began demanding changes. They tried to form unions that could negotiate for better wages and working conditions but faced stiff opposition from owners and managers who wanted to keep operating costs down. In 1914 the

In the late 1800s and early 1900s mining was an important industry in Utah.

attention of workers around the world focused on Utah when Joe Hill, a Swedish immigrant who was a member of the Industrial Workers of the World union, was arrested for shooting two people during a robbery attempt. Although the poems and songs Hill wrote while in prison awaiting trial won him sympathy, he was found guilty and executed. The evidence suggests that Hill did commit the crime, but many observers felt that his trial was conducted unfairly because he was a foreigner and a labor-union member.

While World War I raged overseas from 1914 to 1918, demand for Utah's farm and factory products kept the state's economy humming.

After the war, however, the economy slumped. The decline got worse in 1929 when a severe economic depression gripped the nation. The Great Depression struck especially hard at Utah, which suffered one of the country's highest unemployment rates. During the worst of it, almost 36 percent of Utah's workers were jobless. Not until the United States entered World War II in December 1941 did the state's economy fully recover.

POPULATION GROWTH: 1860–2000

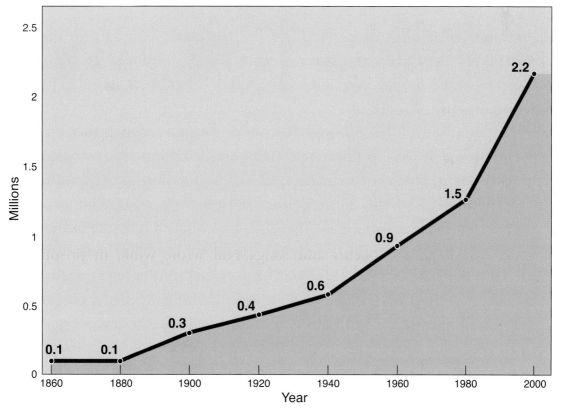

THE WAR EFFORT

More than 71,000 Utahns served in the military during World War II. Within the state there were numerous projects and sites involved in supporting the war effort as well. Utah's vast empty lands were perfect for new and expanded military installations. In 1940 the Army Air Force began using Hill Field as a supply depot and repair center. The Odgen Arsenal had been created in 1921 as a storage facility, but it started actually producing ammunition during the war. A parcel of land around Wendover near the border with Nevada was used for bombing practice. Weapons were also tested at the Dugway Proving Ground near the Great Salt Lake Desert.

Many Utahns also worked in factories that made materials for the armed forces. In Orem, the Geneva Steel Works employed as many as 4,200 people to produce steel plates and other steel items. The Remington Arms Company in Salt Lake County built a factory to produce ammunition for 30- and 50-caliber weapons, which brought ten thousand new jobs to the state. The booming defense industry led to a more than 25 percent increase in Utah's population in the 1940s, attracting more minorities to the state.

After the Japanese attack on the U.S. naval base in Pearl Harbor, Hawaii, the U.S. government decided to detain some Japanese and Japanese Americans at several different sites. Utah was home to one of the facilities where these people were confined, and many of the camp's occupants came from the San Francisco, California, area. After the Topaz internment camp opened in September 1942, about eight thousand internees were housed there, working at jobs on the site or attending one of the makeshift schools there. Living conditions in the desert camp were very difficult, with hot summers and brutal winters.

In 1943 some of the internees could leave if they joined a special military unit. Others were allowed to go if they had someone to sponsor them, but the camp itself did not shut down until October 1945. In the 1980s the U.S. govern-

During World War II some Japanese and Japanese Americans were held in internment camps.

ment apologized for the unfair imprisonment of the internees. Today there are efforts underway to create a museum on part of the Topaz camp's former site to educate people about this painful chapter in American history.

LAND OF CHAMPIONS

Decades after the war ended, Utahns banded together again to prepare for an international sporting event. The Salt Lake City area was selected in 1995 as the site for the 2002 Winter Olympic Games. As soon as the state learned that it was to host the games, it began the necessary preparations. Roughly $1 billion alone was spent reconstructing Interstate 15 to handle all of the anticipated visitors and athletes.

Unfortunately, reports surfaced in 1999 that some members of the Salt Lake City Olympic bid committee had tried to win over the International Olympic Committee using bribes. These allegations cast a cloud over the efforts to get ready for the Olympics. In 2000 two leading members of the Salt Lake City Olympic bid committee were indicted on federal charges related to the bribery scandal, but the case was later dismissed.

In the wake of these allegations, several officials resigned and Massachusetts businessman Mitt Romney stepped in to become the chief executive officer of the Salt Lake Olympic Committee. Romney helped attract new sponsors to the games, such as fast food giant McDonald's, to support the state's Olympic efforts. True to their generous nature, roughly 22,000 Utahns rolled up their sleeves to pitch in and volunteer at the games. On February 8, 2002, the world tuned in to see the opening ceremony for the Winter Olympic Games at the Rice-Eccles Stadium at the University of Utah. A recorded 2,399 athletes from seventy-seven countries came to Utah to compete in seventy-eight events.

While the games ended on February 24, 2002, the Olympics left a lasting impression on Utah. They enabled the state to build new facilities and to enhance existing ones in the Salt Lake City area, including the Utah Olympic Oval in Kearns, the sports arena created for the speed-skating competitions.

Perhaps more importantly, the games helped change the way the world saw the state. "As an Olympic host, Salt Lake City demonstrated its ability to host

All eyes were on Utah as it hosted the 2002 Olympic Winter Games.

major world-class events, and boasts an Olympic legacy of sporting, tourism, and municipal infrastructure," said Melinda McKay of Jones Lang LaSalle, an international real estate and investment company that studied the economic impact of the Olympics.

A NEW ERA

With the same intrepid spirit that drove the Olympic effort, Utah continues to tackle and overcome major challenges. The rising cost of fuel and the nation's unsteady economic times have led to some creative thinking by state officials. In June 2008 Governor Jon Huntsman announced that most government employees would move to a new work schedule, replacing the traditional eight-hour day, five days a week program with a ten-hour day, four days system.

The state expects that this program—called Working 4 Utah—will improve access to government services and programs while cutting costs. "As we go forward with this initiative, we will conserve energy, save money, improve our air quality, and enhance customer service," says Huntsman. The initiative is expected to save the state about $3 million per year in building operation costs, such as utilities. For employees, the cost savings should be even greater—$6 million per year in transportation-related costs.

In addition to cost savings, Working 4 Utah is expected to reduce carbon monoxide emissions by decreasing the number of vehicles on the road. And with government offices open from 7:00 a.m. to 6:00 p.m., Utahns can now visit officials before and after their own workdays.

Widely known for its colorful pioneer past, Utah is proving itself to be a source of innovative and imaginative solutions for the needs of today and tomorrow.

Chapter Three

Life in the Beehive State

In recent years people have flocked to Utah to enjoy its lower cost of living and easy access to all sorts of outdoor activities. Growing nearly 30 percent from 1990 to 2000, the state's population increased from 1.7 million people to 2.3 million, according to the U.S. Census Bureau. The latest report estimates the state's population at 2.6 million and growing fast.

Most Utahns live in or around Salt Lake City. More than two million people live in Salt Lake County and nearby Utah, Davis, and Weber counties. Utah also has the distinction of being the youngest state in the nation, with a median age of 28.4 years, much lower than the national figure of 36.4 years.

While the state's culture has evolved since its early days, Utah's population still closely resembles its first settlers. They were all of one faith, and almost all were white and of northern European descent. Religious, racial, and ethnic diversity have increased a bit since then, but the state is still 93.5 percent white. A recent study from the Pew Forum on Religion & Public Life indicated that Mormons

Whether you're traveling to Utah or you live there, you have many outdoor activities to choose from.

make up about 58 percent of the state's inhabitants today. Once about 70 percent Mormon, Utah is becoming increasingly diverse in terms of religious background.

The state's minority population remains small, but it is growing. American Indians make up about 1.3 percent of Utah residents. There are slightly more Asian Americans at 2 percent, while the number of African Americans stands at only 1 percent. Hispanic Americans, meanwhile, are an expanding section of the state's population. More than 11 percent of Utahns have indicated that they are of Hispanic origin, according to U.S. Census figures. What was once viewed as the Mormons' promised land has evolved to a place of opportunity for people from different cultures and races.

Utah has become a place of opportunity for people from many different races and cultures.

ETHNIC UTAH

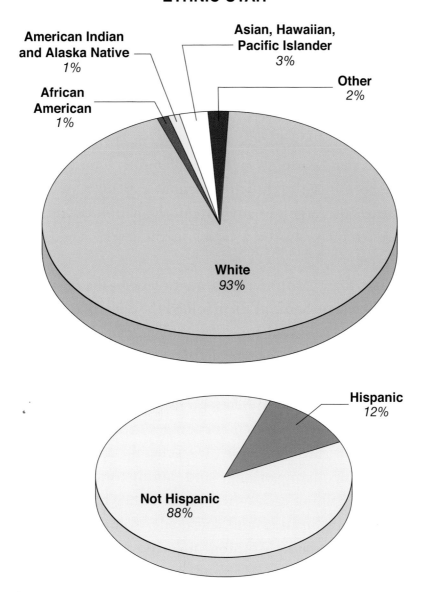

American Indian and Alaska Native
1%

Asian, Hawaiian, Pacific Islander
3%

African American
1%

Other
2%

White
93%

Hispanic
12%

Not Hispanic
88%

Note: A person of Cuban, Mexican, Puerto Rican, South or Central American, or other Spanish culture or origin, regardless of race, is defined as Hispanic.

THE MORMON HERITAGE

Utah is home to people of many different religions. It has a Roman Catholic cathedral, Protestant churches, Jewish synagogues, and Zen Buddhist meditation centers. Still, the majority of the state remains Mormon, and that is not likely to change anytime soon. "The core LDS population will always be a force here," explains University of Utah sociologist Theresa Martinez.

There are two reasons for the steady growth of the Mormon Church in Utah. One is that Mormons favor large families, which means that lots of babies are born into the church. This may explain why Utah's average household size is the largest of any state in the nation, according to 2000 census figures. It may also be a factor in the state's having one of the highest birth rates.

In addition, many Mormons relocate to Utah—the heartland of their faith—from elsewhere. Some of them joined the church as the result of the impelling efforts of Mormon missionaries. The church maintains one of the most active missionary programs in the world today. Many young men and some young unmarried women spend between eighteen months to two years spreading the word about their faith in the United States and abroad.

The qualities that the church encourages in its members contribute to the quality of life in Utah. In general, Mormons are sober, modest, optimistic, hardworking, and family oriented, with strong commitments to helping each other. Because they have a reputation for sticking together in business and social life, some non-Mormons can feel shut out by the state's Mormon majority. As Utah historian Dean L. May wrote, "Here both Mormons and non-Mormons are prone to quickly stereotyping others after determining the all-important question, 'Are they or aren't they [Mormon]?'"

Some of those stereotypes concern marriage. Mormons are supposed to marry not just for life but "for eternity." They believe that non-Mormons regard marriage and divorce too casually. Some fundamentalist Mormons in Utah and elsewhere in the West still practice polygamy. The church has maintained its official position against polygamy and casts out members who openly enter into plural marriages, but those who follow the custom without the church's blessing still consider themselves true Mormons.

Many non-Mormons share the views of Dale Boucette, a resident in Salt Lake City, who said, "Mormons make good neighbors and good citizens, and I really don't care what they believe or what they do behind closed doors."

Even though there are many different religions in Utah, the majority of the state remains Mormon.

POPULATION DENSITY

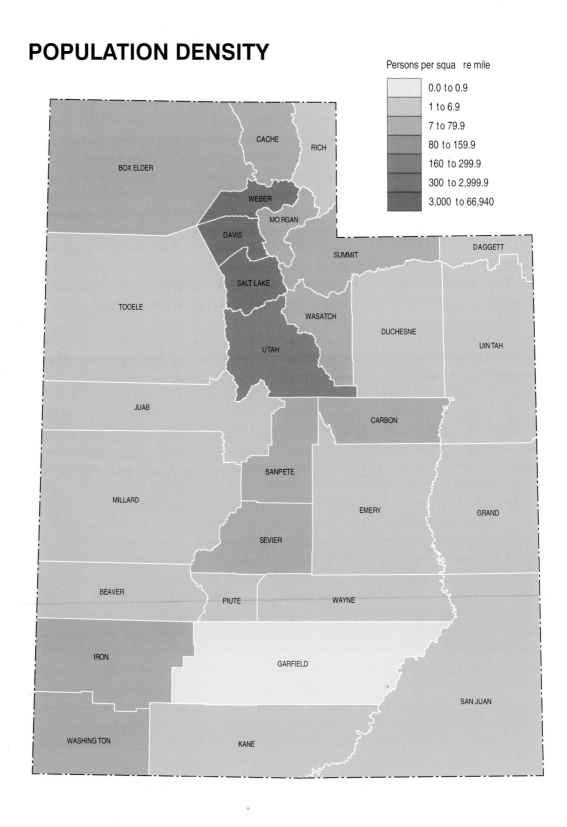

Persons per square mile

- 0.0 to 0.9
- 1 to 6.9
- 7 to 79.9
- 80 to 159.9
- 160 to 299.9
- 300 to 2,999.9
- 3,000 to 66,940

CACHE

RICH

BOX ELDER

WEBER

MO RGAN

DAVIS

SUMMIT

DAGGETT

SALT LAKE

TOOELE

WASATCH

DUCHESNE

UIN TAH

UTAH

JUAB

CARBON

SANPETE

MILLARD

EMERY

GRAND

SEVIER

BEAVER

PIUTE

WAYNE

IRON

GARFIELD

SAN JUAN

WASHING TON

KANE

BEEHIVE STATE HONEY-CARROT CAKE

Honey is one of the many tastes of Utah, and Utahn beekeepers claim that the best honey is made from their state's spring wildflowers. You can enjoy it in this quick, easy, and nutritious cake. Have an adult help you with this recipe.

$1/_2$ cup honey

1 egg

$1/_3$ cup canola oil

1 teaspoon cinnamon

1 teaspoon salt

1 teaspoon vanilla

2 (4.5 ounce) jars strained carrot baby food (it's a lot easier than grating carrots by hand!)

1 $1/_2$ cups all purpose flour

1 teaspoon baking powder

$1/_2$ teaspoon baking soda

$1/_2$ cup golden raisins, chopped nuts, or crushed pineapple (optional)

Start by preheating your oven to 350 °F (177 °C). You will need an 8-inch square baking pan with a nonstick surface, or put parchment paper in the bottom of the pan.

In a large bowl, mix together the honey, egg, canola oil, cinnamon, salt, and vanilla. Then add the carrots. Next, blend in the flour, baking powder, and baking soda. For a chewier cake add the raisins, nuts, or pineapple—or all three.

Pour the batter into the pan and bake it for forty to forty-five minutes. Test to see if the cake is done by sticking a toothpick into the center. If the toothpick comes out clean, the cake is ready to come out of the oven. Let it cool, and then enjoy it, plain or topped with powdered sugar, frosting—or a drizzle of Utah honey.

FROM EUROPE TO UTAH

Non-Mormon immigrants of European descent did not arrive in significant numbers in Utah until the 1860s. The first came to build railroads and work in mines and ore smelters. American companies advertised for workers in foreign cities. Often these workers arrived in the United States unable to speak any English, carrying only a piece of paper with "Salt Lake City" printed on it as a guide to their destination.

Immigrants from Italy began arriving in the 1870s. Some of the early Italian immigrants converted to Mormonism and became rural farmers. But most worked in mines in Bingham, Stockton, and Mercur, where Catholic churches were built. Since then, Italian-American neighborhoods have faded away as the descendants of the immigrants have blended into the larger population.

The next wave of immigrants came from Eastern Europe, followed by those from Greece. By 1910 Greeks were the largest immigrant group in Utah. Greek Americans held on to their cultural identity, partly through participation in their national religion. The first Greek Orthodox church in Utah was built in Salt Lake City in 1905. This and other Greek Orthodox churches became centers of ethnic identity as well as religious worship.

By 1905 thousands of Greeks had arrived in Utah, and in that year they built their first Greek Orthodox church.

Many Utahns continue to honor their Greek heritage in the state today. Every year, such communities as Price and Salt Lake City hold festivals to celebrate Greek culture. Attendees can sample stuffed grape leaves and other Greek favorites, and see dancers perform in traditional clothing.

AMERICAN INDIANS IN UTAH

Before the Mormon settlers and the other Europeans arrived in Utah, five American-Indian peoples called the area home: the Ute, the Paiute, the Shoshone, the Goshute, and the Navajo. While American Indians are only a small fraction of the state's population today, they remain a vibrant force within Utah.

The Navajo, or Diné, as they call themselves (also spelled Dineh), are the largest group in the state, with a population of more than 16,400 in 2006, according to the U.S. Census Bureau. Many of those live on the Navajo Reservation, which is located in the southwestern part of the state and extends into Arizona and New Mexico. At more than 17.2 million acres (7 million ha), the reservation is larger than many U.S. states.

After losing much of their traditional homelands, the Northern Ute were placed on the Uintah and Ouray Indian Reservation. Today the reservation covers more than 4.5 million acres (1.8 million ha) in the northeast part of the state known as the Uinta Basin. More than half of the tribe's 3,157 members reside on the reservation. To support itself, the tribe operates a number of businesses and leases out some of its lands for oil and gas exploration.

The Goshute have two small reservations in the western part of the state: one that extends past the Nevada border and another in Skull Valley. The Skull Valley Band has more than 120 members and has tried to develop businesses related to waste storage and testing facilities. In recent years the band was divided over proposals to use some of their lands to store nuclear waste. To the west of Skull Valley, the Confederated Tribes of the Go-shute Indian Reservation operates a hunting service for interested visitors and is exploring ways to enter the energy marketplace. About ninety people live on their 112,870-acre (45,677-ha) reservation.

After being taken off the list of federally recognized tribes in 1954, the Paiute battled for years to regain their lands and their official status. Their relationship with the federal government was restored in 1980, and some of their lands were returned to them four years later.

Shoshone children perform traditional dances, such as the butterfly dance, during celebrations.

Around 270 people live on the tribe's reservation in Utah.

The Northwestern Band of the Shoshone Nation also has a reservation in the state, which is made up of lands given to them by the LDS church in 1989. Two years earlier they had achieved federal recognition as an individual tribe, independent from other Shoshone groups. The tribe members live in northern Utah and southern Idaho.

Many of the state's native peoples take time each year to keep their rich traditions alive through celebrations and festivals. In June the Paiute Tribal Restoration and Gathering Pow Wow takes place in Cedar City, and the Ute Indian Tribe Pow Wow is held in Fort Duchesne the following month. Many different groups come together for the Native American Association Festival and Contest Pow Wow in Salt Lake City every August.

AFRICAN AMERICANS IN UTAH

Over the years there has been some speculation about why the state's African-American population has remained so small. Many believe one reason is that the Mormon faith has not attracted many black believers. Some of the first African Americans arrived in Utah as slaves to southern Mormons in the late 1840s. Also around that time, the first free blacks—the James family—joined other Mormon settlers in their new homeland.

The railroad and mining industries drew more African Americans to the state in the late 1800s. While some African Americans helped build the railroad lines, more found jobs as porters, waiters, and other related positions aboard the trains and in the hotels along the lines. Black members of the Ninth Calvary—known as buffalo soldiers—came to Utah's Fort Duchesne in 1886. Ten years later, more African-American soldiers were stationed at Fort Douglas in Salt Lake City.

By the beginning of the twentieth century, a small but vibrant African-American community had developed in Salt Lake City. Still, African Americans faced discrimination within the state, including restricted access to housing and segregation of some public spaces. As with the rest of the nation, the civil rights movement of the 1960s helped bring equalizing changes to the state.

In 1972 Donald Cope was selected by Governor Calvin Rampton to become the state's first ombudsman—an official who investigates complaints and tries to resolve disputes—for the African-American community. Four years later, Robert Harris made history as the first African American elected to the state legislature. Terry Williams achieved a similar milestone in 1980 as the first African American to serve in the Utah senate. In addition to the crumbling of political barriers, African Americans saw another restriction lifted in 1976 when the LDS church ended its ban on male blacks joining the priesthood.

Over time, African Americans have come to Utah for many reasons. Today they generally come in search of professional employment opportunities.

Each January, African Americans across the state honor the memory of slain civil rights leader Rev. Martin Luther King Jr. Held on the third Monday in January, this holiday became an official part of the state's calendar in 1986. Special events, such as public rallies and services, take place to celebrate King's life and work on this day.

While not an official state holiday, Juneteenth is another important celebration for African-American Utahns. It marks an important event in the history of slavery in the United States. Abraham Lincoln had freed all of the slaves with the Emancipation Proclamation in 1863, but it took until after the end of the Civil War for this freedom to become a reality for many. When Union forces reached Galveston, Texas, on June 19, 1865, they brought with them the news that all of the slaves were now free. One of the state's largest celebrations of Juneteenth is held in Ogden and features music, food, and educational programs. "It's just a great reason to bring families together and remember the past. And remember it's not just African Americans' past, but everybody's past," said event attendee Stuart Michaels.

ASIAN AMERICANS IN UTAH

Asians make up about 2 percent of the state's population. Some of the first Asians to arrive were the Chinese in the 1860s and 1870s. Many Chinese workers came to the state as construction workers, helping to build the Central Pacific Railroad line from Sacramento, California, to Promontory, Utah. Some stayed on and settled in Box Elder County and continued working for the railroad.

By the 1890s, most of Utah's Chinese residents had moved to neighborhoods in Salt Lake City, Ogden, and Park City. Merchants, such as Wong Leung Ka in Ogden, set up shops to cater to the needs of their fellow immigrants. These communities flourished for a time, but the Great Depression of the 1930s led to a decline in the Chinese population.

Since the end of World War II, however, many Chinese immigrants have decided to make Utah their home. There are a number of Chinese community organizations in the state today, and many of them work together to hold special events and celebrations. One of the most popular is the Chinese New Year celebration held in Salt Lake City, which includes martial arts demonstrations, Chinese music, and children's dances.

The Japanese are another leading group in the state's Asian population. The first Japanese immigrants arrived in the 1880s. After 1890 the Hashimoto family of Salt Lake City became a leading supplier of labor to western railroads and industries. Although the Japanese came originally as laborers, many of them stayed on as truck farmers, growing celery and strawberries in Salt Lake, Weber, and Box Elder counties.

Today Japanese Utahns honor their heritage through special events, such as

Chinese New Year is a celebration that extends for many days, ending with the Golden Dragon Parade.

the Obon Dance Festival at the Salt Lake Buddhist Temple. Each year attendees enjoy Japanese foods such as chicken teriyaki, listen to traditional taiko drums, and learn folk dances. "It started out as a Japanese Buddhist tradition and grew into a Japanese-American custom. Now it appeals to the community as a whole," explains Brenda Koga, chairwoman of the 2008 Obon Festival.

HISPANIC AMERICANS IN UTAH

Hispanic Americans are the state's fastest-growing minority. Initially Utah was only a part of the way for Spanish explorers Francisco Domínguez and

Silvestre Vélez de Escalante in 1776 as their party searched for a route between New Mexico and California. That expedition failed as winter weather forced their return to Santa Fe. By the early nineteenth century, however, a well-used trail that passed through Utah linked the two areas.

By the end of the 1800s, Hispanic Americans had moved from New Mexico into the San Juan County area, especially at Monticello, where they worked as sheepherders and ranch hands. In the northern part of the state, workers from Mexico landed jobs with the railroad and in the area's mines. Some ventured into Carbon County to work in the coal mines there.

During World War II more Hispanic Americans moved into the state to work in the state's booming defense industry. Many Hispanics today are still drawn to the state for the economic opportunities it presents as well as the state's reputation for being family oriented. "Utah is one of the best states for raising children, and I think that's why it has been growing a lot," explains Manuel Velasco, who moved to Utah from Mexico with his family in 1995.

There have been some lingering tensions between the state's white majority and the Hispanic community over such issues as immigration and political representation. All parties, nonetheless, put their differences aside for such holidays as Cinco de Mayo. This holiday celebrates the victory of Mexican forces over French troops at the Battle of Puebla on May 5, 1862. Over the years the celebration has evolved. "It's become more of a cultural, commercial pheno-menon in terms of building awareness and educating the public about the Mexican culture," explains John Renteria, director of Salt Lake City's Centro Civico Mexicano. The festivities held throughout the state usually include dancing, mariachi music, and lots of delicious food.

Cities and towns decorate their streets and homes with flowers, while enjoying music, food, and games, to celebrate Cinco de Mayo.

THE STATE OF EDUCATION

No matter what their background, Utahns are proud of their state's educational achievements. The emphasis on learning can be traced back to the early days of the Mormon faith. Brigham Young said, "Education is the power to think clearly, to act well in the day's work, and to appreciate life." About 94 percent of adult Utahns can read and write, giving the state one of the highest literacy rates in the nation. The Utah ranks second in the nation in the percentage of adults who have graduated from high school.

Yet Utah's schools are not without problems. With 31 percent of the state's population under the age of eighteen, its education system has been stretched to fit the needs of an ever-growing population. Utah spends much less than other states on each pupil. For the 2005–2006 school year, the state spent an average of $5,437 per student, about $3,701 less than the national average of $9,138, according to a report from the Utah Foundation. While reduced spending does not necessarily affect the quality of the state's educational programs, it can lead to larger class sizes and difficulty in hiring and retaining skilled teachers. In Utah, there is, on average, 1 teacher for every 22.1 students, noticeably larger than the national average of 1 teacher for 15.7 students.

Teachers' salaries are another issue in the state. According to a survey by the American Federation of Teachers, Utah was one of the lowest-paying states in the nation, with an average salary of $37,006, for the 2004–2005 school year. The state government has been working to improve teachers' compensation since then. In 2007 teachers received a $2,500 boost to their base pay. "Quality education is driven by quality teachers," explains Governor Jon Huntsman. Hopefully these increases will help the state attract more competent teachers.

Chapter Four
Land of Laws

When Mormon settlers began arriving in Utah in 1847, they dreamed of creating a society whose government and economy would be shaped by the church. The Mormons developed their own political system, the State of Deseret, which lasted until 1870. To become a part of the United States, however, they had to make changes to that early vision. Utah's government now operates like those of the other forty-nine states, and its economy is intertwined with that of the rest of the nation and the world.

INSIDE GOVERNMENT

The government of Utah, like the federal government, consists of three branches—executive, legislative, and judicial—that perform different functions.

Executive

The executive branch is responsible for putting the state's laws and policies into action. It is headed by the governor, who is elected to a four-year term. Other executive officials are the lieutenant governor,

Completed in 1916, the Utah State Capitol houses both branches of the state legislature, which are the senate and the house of representatives.

who takes over if the governor cannot fulfill his or her duties, and the state's attorney general, treasurer, and auditor. Various departments and agencies oversee a host of government services, such as education, tax collection, environmental protection, and road maintenance. Some officials who administer these services are elected, while the governor appoints others.

Legislative

The legislative branch makes the state laws. It consists of a senate and a house of representatives. The twenty-nine senators serve four-year terms; the seventy-five representatives serve two-year terms. They develop bills that propose new laws or change existing laws and then vote on whether to make the bills into laws. If both houses pass a bill it goes to the governor, who can either sign it into law or turn it down by vetoing it. A bill vetoed by the governor can still become law if two-thirds of the legislature votes for it.

Judicial

The judicial branch is responsible for hearing legal cases and interpreting state laws. There are three sets of trial courts: district courts for serious cases; justice courts where justices of the peace hear minor cases; and juvenile courts for cases involving young people. Someone not satisfied with the verdict of one of these lower courts can ask the court of appeals to hear the case. The court of appeals consists of seven judges who serve six-year terms. Appeals from this court go to Utah's five-member supreme court, which also rules on whether or not laws conform to the state's constitution. The governor appoints the supreme court justices to ten-year terms, but they must be approved by the voters in the next general election.

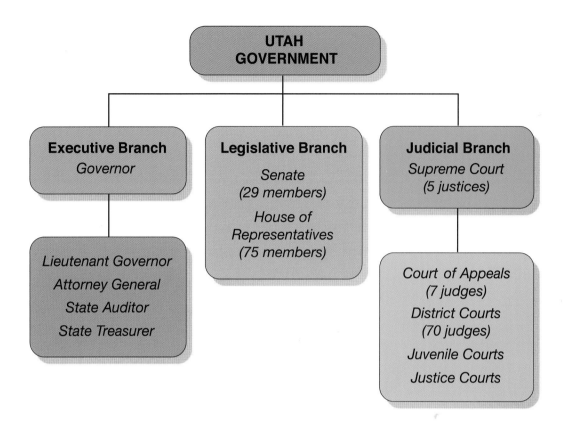

UTAH GOVERNMENT

Executive Branch
Governor

Lieutenant Governor
Attorney General
State Auditor
State Treasurer

Legislative Branch
Senate
(29 members)

House of Representatives
(75 members)

Judicial Branch
Supreme Court
(5 justices)

Court of Appeals
(7 judges)
District Courts
(70 judges)
Juvenile Courts
Justice Courts

A POLITICAL PIONEER

Even before becoming a state, Utah proved itself to be a maker of progressive laws, especially related to women's rights. The legislature of the Utah Territory gave women the right to vote in 1870. Two years later the Married Person's Property Act of 1872 enabled wives to have control over real estate they owned before they were wed. The federal government, unfortunately, took away Utah women's voting rights in 1887.

After several tries, Utah was finally admitted into the Union in 1896, becoming the forty-fifth state. Its state constitution, passed in 1895, included the restoration of women's voting rights. Utahn women wasted no time enjoying their newly regained rights. In 1896 Martha Hughes Cannon became the first woman elected to a state senate. As a legislator, she worked to create a state board of health.

In 1992 Olene S. Walker became Utah's first female lieutenant governor. She later assumed the role of governor in 2003 from Governor Michael Okerlund Leavitt when he resigned to head up the Environmental Protection Agency. During her time as Utah's first female governor, Walker worked on many issues, including health, education, and the environment. She helped develop wellness and reading programs as well as natural resources management projects.

Olene S. Walker became the state's first female governor in 2003.

UTAH BY COUNTY

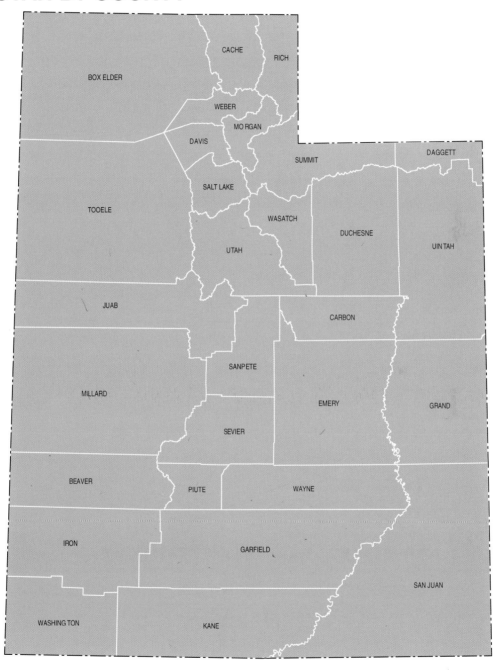

PROTECTING THE PAST

Through the years Utah has juggled the needs of the present with broad appeal to maintain its storied past. The state legislature showed its commitment to preserving history with the passage of the Utah Antiquities Act in 1973. The law created a new section within the Division of State History to protect prehistoric sites and artifacts discovered in the state. Called the State Antiquities Section, it became responsible for organizing and recording information about these sites and discoveries.

The Utah Antiquities Act was passed in 1973. This law protects prehistoric sites and artifacts discovered in the state of Utah.

This section was also established to encourage research in the areas of archaeology and anthropology and to publish its findings.

The state also gained its own archaeologist through this act. As part of the position, the archaeologist was able to create a staff to help carry out policies established by the Division of State History. Some of its most important powers related to land use. With the act, permits were now required to enter a designated site on state land. Even permitted archaeologists and researchers had to follow certain guidelines, and any artifacts recovered became property of the state. In that way, Utah was able to prevent treasures from its own past from leaving the state. Certain places could also be declared state archaeological or anthropological landmarks—but only with the landowner's consent for private property.

The act also required that any discoveries of an archaeological or anthropological nature made on state land must be reported to the Division of State History. It declared illegal the destruction of prehistoric sites or specimens, as well as the removal of artifacts. Counterfeiting of artifacts also became a state crime.

Decades earlier the federal government had established its own protective law with the Antiquities Act of 1906. That law was also designed to preserve historic sites and artifacts in the West. Over the years, many U.S. presidents have used this act to create national monuments, such as the Grand Canyon in 1908 (it became a national park in 1919). President Franklin D. Roosevelt also expanded the Dinosaur National Monument on the Utah-Colorado border in 1938. Perhaps the most strongly contested use of the Antiquities Act happened in 1996 when President Bill Clinton established the Grand Staircase–Escalante National Monument in southwestern Utah.

FIGHT OVER LAND

Like other western states, Utah includes a great deal of land owned and managed by federal agencies such as the Bureau of Land Management and the U.S. Forest Service. More than 67 percent of Utah is federal land. Utah has taken a leading role in what some call the "sagebrush rebellion," efforts by western states to gain greater control over the use of federal land and resources.

In 1996 one of the most heated debates raged in Utah over the creation of the Grand Staircase–Escalante National Monument. Some Utahns were strongly opposed to monument status for this Delaware-size piece of desert. Although the Bureau of Land Management still administers the land—as it did before—the region's status as a national monument means more restrictions. For instance, a Dutch corporation had to halt plans for large-scale coal mining in the monument, enraging Utahns who expected the mining operation to be a source of income. Senator Orrin Hatch of Utah called the monument a federal land grab, even though the land already belonged to the federal government, not to the state, before it was designated into a monument. A local politician compared the establishment of the monument to the "invasion" of 1857, despite the fact that grazing and hunting can freely continue within the monument.

But Ross "Rocky" Anderson, a Salt Lake City politician, argues that many Utahns want to see their land protected. "The view that all Utahns are up in arms because of the designation of this national monument is a horrible misconception," he says. "Most people love this state because of the incredible beauty."

The Utah Antiquities Act has also had to weather a number of challenges over the years. With the increasing demand for land and natural resources, there have been many efforts to change the act. The State Antiquities and Historic Sites Amendments of 2006 made a dramatic alteration to the Antiquities Section. All the permits are now handled by the Public Lands Policy Coordinating Office instead of the Antiquities Section. The act's sponsor, State Representative Bradley T. Johnson, said that "the archaeological people out there are kind of prone to protect every site, at all cost." The Public Lands Policy Coordinating Office "has the ability to make a more balanced judgment," he explains.

Not everyone agrees with Representative Johnson's point of view, though. A letter issued by the Utah Professional Archaeological Council stated its objections to giving the control of permits to the Public Lands Policy Coordinating Office. It claimed that Utah is putting some of its most valuable assets at risk, since the office does not have appropriately trained staff for managing historic sites and artifacts. "Historical and archaeological resources are irreplaceable remains of our cultural heritage," the letter explained. As long as Utah maintains its strong growth rate, the conflict between preserving the past and building for the future will continue.

Historic sites, such as Fruita, where early Mormons settled, are considered important artifacts and remind Utahns of their past.

TAKING THE INITIATIVE

Legislators may make many of the laws, but the people of Utah have the power to question those laws. In a referendum, voters can approve or reject a law passed by the state legislature. Other times the people themselves want to create new laws for the state. Called an initiative, such a proposed law is put on the election ballot to allow voters to decide whether or not it should become part of the state's legal code.

Initiatives appear on the ballot more often than referendums. For an initiative to be put to a vote, interested citizens must follow a number of steps, including submitting an application and circulating a petition. Sponsors of the initiative have to get enough voters to sign the petition for it to be approved; they need at least 10 percent of the total number of voters from last gubernatorial election.

Utahns take their initiatives seriously. More than 130,000 citizens signed the petition to put the Utah Clean Water, Quality Growth and Open Space Initiative on the 2004 election ballot. Through this proposed legislation, the state would have created a $150 million bond to be used to buy land, such as farmland, animal habitats, and watershed areas, to be preserved as open space. Utah residents would have experienced a small sales tax increase to make this bond possible. At election time, they made their wishes perfectly clear, with 55 percent of the voters rejecting the initiative. Many experts reasoned that voters supported the need for open space but did not like the idea of paying more in taxes.

In 2007 the state's voters tackled their first referendum since 1974. A referendum can only be called after a petition has been circulated and all of the necessary signatures—the same amount required for an initiative—

have been collected and submitted to the state. Through this bill, public school students would be able to attend certain private schools using scholarships provided by the state. Families were to receive between five hundred and three thousand dollars per child for private school education, depending on the family's size and their income.

For many years, school vouchers have been a subject of debate in many states across the country. Its advocates say vouchers give parents the opportunity to choose what is best for their children. On the other side of the debate, its opponents claim that vouchers may undermine the public school system by diverting funds from state schools or lead to a tax increase to support both the current system and the school voucher program. The majority of Utah voters—62 percent—decided that this program was not right for their state.

Chapter Five

A Changing Economy

In the early days of the state, Utahns made their living from the land and its natural resources. While farming and mining continue to thrive there, most residents work in service-related jobs, from health care to education to sales. Overall, the state has a much lower unemployment rate—around 3.5 percent in 2008—than the national average of more than 6.5 percent.

Much of the state's success can be attributed to its inhabitants' strong work ethic, reflecting after the Utah symbol, the beehive. The Mormon settlers chose the beehive because bees are industrious and work together for the common good, and Utahns continue to follow their example. It's no wonder that the business news cable network CNBC picked Utah as number three on its list of top states for business in 2008.

LIVING OFF THE LAND

While most Utahns live and work in its cities, there are still some who engage in traditional agricultural work in rural areas. Many of the state's farms can be found in Beaver, Utah, Box Elder, Millard, and Cache counties. With more than 11 million acres (4.5 million ha) of land in

Some Utahns, such as this beekeeper, work in the agricultural industry.

Utah used for agriculture, most of these areas are pastures for the state's prime agricultural commodity, cattle. Dairy products, hogs, and hay are other important farm products.

Farmers also grow a variety of crops there, including wheat, barley, oats, corn, and potatoes. Some tend to orchards filled with apple, apricot, and cherry trees—just some of the fruits produced in Utah. And just like the state symbol, some farmers tend to beehives to produce and collect honey.

Utah, however, is more famous for what comes out of its lands than what grows on them. Since the discovery of silver and gold in 1860s, mining has been a part of the state's economy. Some early miners sought gold, silver, and copper. Others worked on digging up coal. For a brief while during the 1950s, until the market for this radioactive material faded, uranium was one of the state's top mining products.

Some Utahns still work on unearthing minerals and metals today. The state is the fourth-largest producer of nonfuel minerals in the country and the second-largest producer of copper and gold. Kennecott Copper Mine,

southwest of Salt Lake City, is one of the largest open-pit mines in the world. While the number of mines in the state dropped in recent years, ten active mines produced more than 24 tons of coal in 2007. In addition to mining coal, Utahns also work in the production of other energy products, including oil and natural gas.

The Kennecott Copper Mine is so large that it can be seen from space.

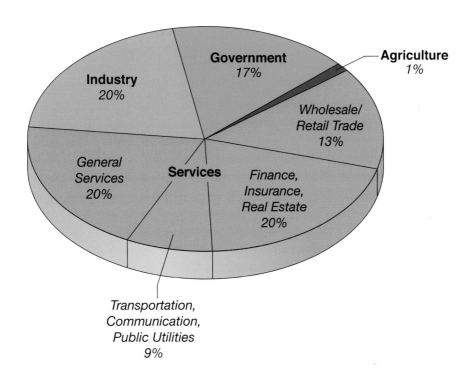

2007 GROSS STATE PRODUCT: $106 Million

- Government 17%
- Agriculture 1%
- Industry 20%
- Wholesale/Retail Trade 13%
- General Services 20%
- Services
- Finance, Insurance, Real Estate 20%
- Transportation, Communication, Public Utilities 9%

GOING HIGH TECH

While supporting its traditional industries, such as mining, Utah is working to develop its technology sector. The computer, aerospace, and medical industries are the leading high-tech segments in the state. More than 1,800 companies provide information technology products and services. While there are some bigger players, such as software developer Novell in Provo, most computer-related businesses in the state have less than fifty employees.

Unlike the computer-related fields, the aerospace industry has fewer businesses in the state, but they are usually much larger in size. One of the biggest aerospace employers is ATK Space Systems, part of the Minnesota-based Alliant Techsystems. It has facilities in Brigham City and Magna and develops products related to missile systems and space travel.

The state has a long history with cultivating innovation, especially in the field of medicine. In 1968 the state legislature approved the creation of the University of Utah Research Park. That productive facility has helped create many businesses based on the work of university scientists and experts over the years. One such collaboration, the Artificial Heart Test Evaluation, led to the development of a permanent artificial heart, the Jarvik 7, which was named after its creator Dr. Robert Jarvik. In 1982 Barney Clark, at the University of Utah, became the first person to have this device surgically implanted in his body. The University of Utah Research Park now houses more than forty companies alongside sixty-nine academic departments and employs more than 7,500 people. Still other research parks have been formed in the state to turn academic discoveries into business success stories.

SUPPORTING THE STATE

With the state's growing population, it is no wonder that the careers of many Utahns revolve around the care and education of fellow residents. One of the state's largest employers is Intermountain Healthcare, with more than 20,000 people on its payroll. Other major job providers include Brigham Young University, the University of Utah, Utah State University, and several of the state's largest school districts, such as Granite, Jordan, and Davis County school districts.

Other Utahns work in retail sales, helping people get the consumer goods they need for their everyday lives. Wal-Mart Stores, Inc., the grocery chains Albertsons and the Kroger Group Company, and Home Depot are just three of the large retail employers in the state. Some help with financial matters, such as the employees of Zions First National Bank, another important Utah company.

In the coming years, the state expects to see demand for certain service industry jobs to increase. More people will be needed in computer- and medical-related occupations, such as software engineers and home health-care aides, especially in Utah's urban areas. In more rural locales the number of positions available for medical and public safety personnel, such as registered nurses and firefighters, will likely be growing.

Jobs in the medical-related industry, such as lab technicians, are expected to increase in Utah.

EARNING A LIVING

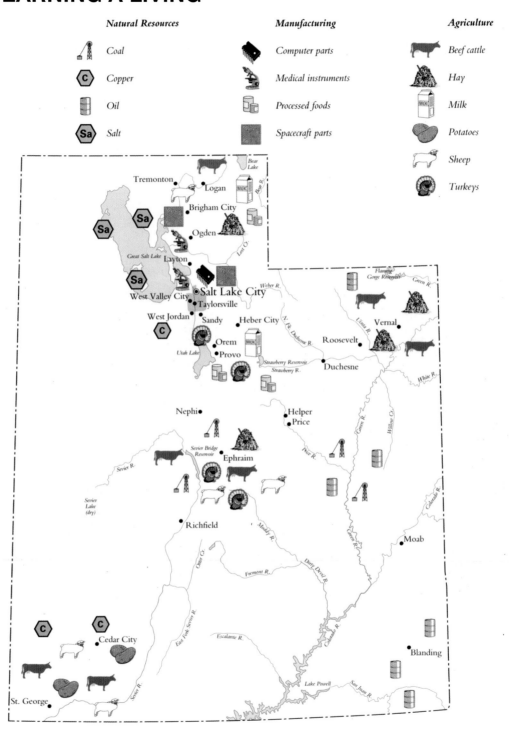

Natural Resources

Coal
C Copper
Oil
Sa Salt

Manufacturing

Computer parts
Medical instruments
Processed foods
Spacecraft parts

Agriculture

Beef cattle
Hay
Milk
Potatoes
Sheep
Turkeys

Bear Lake
Tremonton
Logan
Bear R.
Brigham City
Sa Sa
Ogden
Great Salt Lake Layton
Lost Cr.
Weber R.
Sa Salt Lake City
West Valley City Taylorsville
West Jordan
C Sandy Heber City
Orem
Utah Lake Provo
N. Fk. Duchesne R.
Flaming Gorge Reservoir
Green R.
Vernal
Uinta R.
Roosevelt
Strawberry Reservoir
Strawberry R. Duchesne
White R.
Nephi
Helper
Price
Sevier Bridge Reservoir
Ephraim
Sevier R.
Price R.
Cottonwood Cr.
Willow Cr.
Sevier Lake (dry)
Richfield
Muddy R.
Green R.
Colorado R.
Moab
Otter Cr.
Fremont R.
Dirty Devil R.
C C
Cedar City
East Fork Sevier R.
Escalante R.
Colorado R.
Blanding
Sevier R.
Lake Powell
San Juan R.
St. George

DESTINATION UTAH

Travel and tourism has been one of the strongest segments of Utah's economy, bringing in $6 billion in 2007. Making up about 9 percent of all nonfarming related jobs, travel- and tourism-related businesses employ more than 113,000 Utahns. These businesses include transportation companies, restaurants, hotels, car rentals, and entertainment-related businesses.

Outdoor activities are one of the state's leading attractions. As a result, once desolate rural towns have been transformed into tourist destinations. On any weekend as many as ten thousand rafters, hikers, and mountain bikers converge on the tiny town of Moab. This community has greeted the tourist boom with coffee shops, inns, trendy restaurants, outfitters who supply gear to the adventurous, and boutiques where anyone can buy stylish sportswear that at least looks adventurous. "This was a dying uranium town," says a Moab bartender, recalling the days before the boom.

Visitors to the town of Moab enjoy the many great biking trails in the area, including the famous Slickrock trail.

Park City, another former mining town, has become a big draw for skiers and celebrities. Every January the world-famous Sundance Film Festival is held there. Its main streets turn into a mini-Hollywood as movie industry movers and shakers come to preview the latest independent films. Nearby Alta started out as a wild mining town in the late 1800s and has evolved into one of Utah's top ski areas. In all, it has been estimated that the state's thirteen ski resorts did more than $1 billion worth of business in the 2007–2008 ski season. "Utah's incredible snow, unparalleled accessibility and world class resorts continue to attract new visitors, making it a crucial source of revenue for the state," says Nathan Rafferty, president of Ski Utah, which promotes the state's winter tourism.

Tourists visit Park City, Utah, to enjoy many of their ski mountains.

GETTING INTO GEAR

The site of a former trading post used by trappers and settlers, Ogden is now home to many companies that help people have outdoor adventures. Many of these businesses were inspired to move to Ogden by the 2002 Winter Olympic Games, held in the Salt Lake City area. The Snowbasin ski resort, near Ogden, hosted several of the Olympic ski events. The international sport competition put a spotlight on all that northern Utah had to offer as both a business and recreational destination.

One of the early Olympic-related arrivals was Descente North America (DNA), a maker of sports apparel. As Ogden native and vice president of DNA Curt Geiger explains, "If I hadn't come back in 2002 and looked at what they'd done at Snowbasin, I might never have come back."

Other companies have followed in DNA's footsteps. In 2005 Goode Ski Technologies, makers of snow and water skis, ski poles, and accessories, came to the city. The company has stated that the move to Utah was driven by the desire to be closer to world-class snow and water skiing. In 2006 Amer Sports decided to make Ogden the North American head-quarters for its winter and outdoor businesses, which includes such brands as Salomon, Mavic, and Atomic. Many other sports-related companies have offices in Ogden, and the city plans to attract even more.

When the ski season draws to a close, the number of visitors to the state's five national parks begins to climb. Arches, Bryce Canyon, Canyonlands, Capitol Reef, and Zion national parks attracted close to 5.5 million visitors in 2007. Other outdoor adventures can be found in Utah's forty-one state parks, which had approximately 4.7 million visitors that same year.

There are many ways to tour Utah's five national parks, including taking a mule ride.

In addition to skiers, hikers, and other active tourists, Utah has been working hard to lure another kind of visitor—film and television crews. The Utah Film Commission offers these companies special tax breaks and incentives to make their films, shows, and commercials there. More than eight hundred films and television movies have been made in Utah, from the classic 1939 western *Stagecoach* to the 2000 action thriller *Mission Impossible II*. The state has more recently been involved in the hugely popular *High School Musical* phenomena. Utah was also the site for the 2005 television movie as well as the 2008 feature film *High School Musical 3: Senior Year*. Both productions spent more than $15 million in the state.

UTAH WORKFORCE

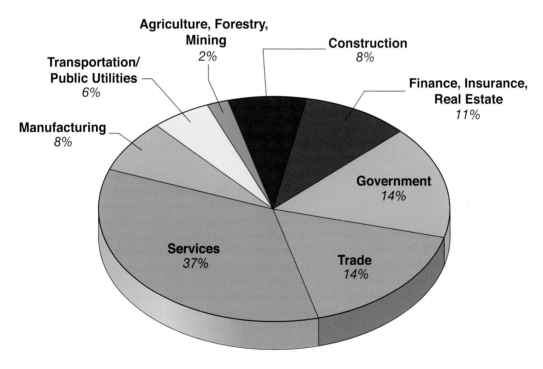

Agriculture, Forestry, Mining
2%

Construction
8%

Transportation/
Public Utilities
6%

Finance, Insurance,
Real Estate
11%

Manufacturing
8%

Government
14%

Services
37%

Trade
14%

SELLING GOODS ABROAD

In addition to its world-famous landscapes, Utah is also known around the globe for its goods. The state has developed strong international business relationships over the years and sold an estimated $7.8 billion in goods to other countries in 2007. Its largest export is gold, making up 40.8 percent of all items sold abroad. In fact, more gold is sold than is actually mined in the state. Mined in other states, gold ore is shipped to Utah for processing, where it is transformed into pure gold. This precious metal accounts for more than 90 percent of goods sold to the United Kingdom, Switzerland, and India. Besides gold, other popular exports include computers and electronics, transportation equipment, and minerals.

Seeking to boost Utah's image abroad, Governor Jon Huntsman traveled to China in 2006. He and other members of the trade mission met with Chinese government officials in Beijing and Shanghai. "I'd have to say this was what I'd consider to be a successful foray. . . . We left a positive impression about the state," said Governor Huntsman. Clearly that impression has paid off, with Utah's exports to China growing from more than $217 million in 2006 to $305 million in 2007. In addition to increased business with China, the state has seen a wider demand for its goods from other parts of Asia.

THE ROAD AHEAD

Beginning in 2006 the nation's economy experienced difficulties because of problems in the housing market. Many people had taken out large mortgages, or loans, to buy new homes, but they had difficulty making their payments. In turn, the mortgage companies had trouble meeting their own financial obligations because they were not collecting money from the homeowners. Some of these companies went bankrupt, causing a national economic crisis.

In Utah the nation's housing situation has contributed to a decline in the construction industry. The number of new single-family home construction permits dropped 20 percent from 26,300 in 2006 to 21,000 in 2007. Nonresidential construction, nonetheless, remains strong as companies move forward with big projects, such as the Intermountain Health Care Southwest Valley Hospital in Riverton. The Church of Jesus Christ of Latter-day Saints is also actively working to renovate several blocks of Salt Lake City, which is expected to cost more than $1.5 billion.

Rising fuel costs have also taken their toll on the nation, driving up the price of some goods and services, such as food and airfare. Like the rest of the nation, Utahns have felt some of this economic sting. State officials and business leaders, however, remain optimistic about Utah's future. While some decline in the rate of growth is expected, they believe that the state will continue to prosper. "Utah's economy has slowed from about 70 to 25 miles per hour (113 to 40 km per hour), while the national economy is parked by the side of the road with a couple of flat tires," says Jeff Thredgold, an economic consultant with Zions Bank and other companies.

No matter what the twenty-first century may bring, Utah will weather any storm with its robust tourist industry and its ability to support existing companies and to attract new businesses.

Chapter Six

Utah Road Trip

Utah has something for everyone. Like history? Visit one of the many museums in Salt Lake City. Rather go on a hike? Try one of Utah's national parks or monuments. Whether you enjoy culture or adventure or awesome natural splendor, you can find what you're looking for while visiting the state.

AROUND SALT LAKE CITY

Temple Square, one of the oldest parts of Salt Lake City, houses the major structures of the Church of Jesus Christ of Latter-day Saints. The square is a place of pilgrimage for Mormons, but many non-Mormons enjoy touring its beautifully maintained gardens and buildings, including the tabernacle. The tabernacle was completed in 1867 and is home to the world-renown Mormon Tabernacle Choir. The impressive Salt Lake Temple itself, however, is open only to those of the Mormon faith.

In and around the square you can also see monuments to the seagulls and the handcart pioneers that played important roles in early Mormon history. A visit to the Beehive House provides a glimpse into

Capitol Reef National Park is filled with fascinating sandstone formations carved into marvelous shapes, which make it an unbelievable adventure for all visitors.

family life of the mid-1800s. With his family, Brigham Young lived in this residence while he was governor of the Utah Territory and during his years as president of the LDS church. Take a walk around the grounds of Temple Square and you are likely to encounter some young Mormons who are eager to answer questions and show visitors around.

Backed by broad mountains that are speckled green with trees and white with snow, Salt Lake City is a handsome place. It's also easy to tour on foot or bicycle. Climb uphill to

The Salt Lake Temple is the largest Mormon temple, and it took forty years to build.

the state capitol for a wide view of the city, and admire the building's copper dome. Inside you'll find murals illustrating key eras and events in the state's history. For another taste of history, drop by the Pioneer Memorial Museum and see displays of memorabilia from some of the state's earliest settlers.

Before leaving the vicinity of Salt Lake City, don't forget to see the Great Salt Lake itself. Depending upon the light, the water appears blue, green, gray, or even maroon—its mineral content gives it such surprising colors. Antelope Island has beaches where you can take a dip. An Oregon couple who did so had two common reactions. One of them exclaimed, "Cool! Look how I'm floating!" The other cried, "Eww! There are little critters in this water, and it's slimy!" Rinse in freshwater as soon as you get out, or you'll itch from the salt for the rest of the day.

Departing Salt Lake City, you may head west for a look at the salt desert and the wide-open spaces of the Basin and Range Province. Or you may choose to go northeast to explore mountain towns, green valleys, and

The Great Salt Lake is one of the largest natural lakes in the country.

the wilderness areas of Rocky Mountain Province. Most visitors, though, head south to Utah's most dramatic geology and its amazing string of five national parks. On the way, stop at Timpanogos Cave National Monument. You'll hike a mile and a half up a mountain to reach the cave, but the climb is scenic and the monument is even better. It consists of three caves linked by narrow tunnels and draped in an amazing variety of crystals and dripstone formations. At roughly 45 °F (7 °C), the cave is a chilly relief on a hot summer day.

Driving through Utah, the surroundings may seem familiar to you, and no wonder—the state's landscapes have served as the background for dozens of television shows and movies. If you can't get to Utah, you can see it in such films as *Planet of the Apes, Butch Cassidy and the Sundance Kid,* and *Independence Day.*

THE SOUTHEAST

Head for Moab, set amid hundreds of square miles of the smoothly curving, polished red sandstone known as slickrock. One of the area's most popular mountain-biking trails takes its name from this beautiful sandstone. Each year more than 100,000 people set out for adventure on the challenging 12-mile (19-km) Slickrock Bike Trail.

At nearby Arches National Park you can hike among enormous rock formations, including more than two thousand natural arches, the remnants of rock walls that have worn away from beneath due to weathering over vast stretches of time. Nowhere in the world can you see more rock arches than in this place. Hike a short way along one of the trails in the late afternoon, then sit in the desert silence to watch the sunset illuminate red rock against a deep blue sky.

Arches National Park is located in southern Utah and is known for over two thousand natural sandstone arches.

PLACES TO SEE

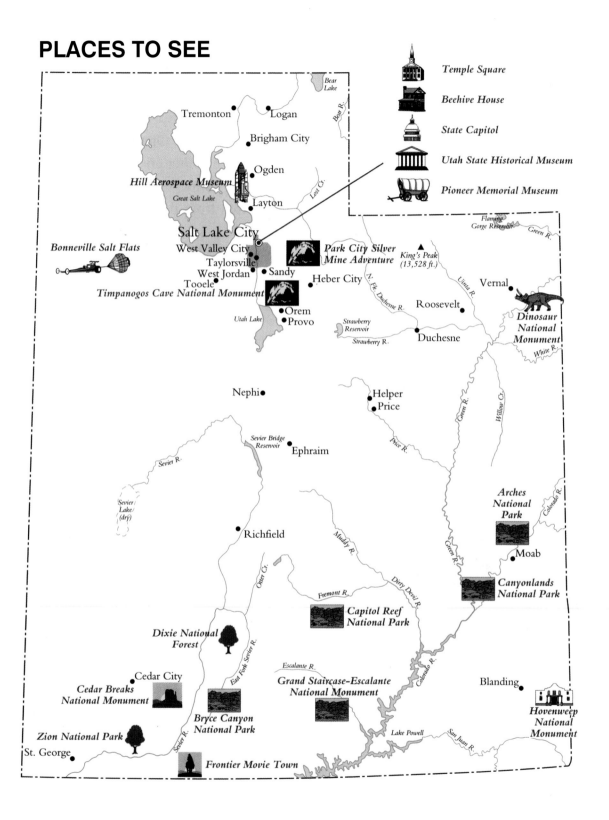

Temple Square

Beehive House

State Capitol

Utah State Historical Museum

Pioneer Memorial Museum

Bear Lake

Tremonton
Logan
Bear R.

Brigham City

Ogden

Hill Aerospace Museum

Great Salt Lake

Layton

Lost Cr.

Flaming Gorge Reservoir
Green R.

Bonneville Salt Flats

Salt Lake City

West Valley City

Taylorsville
West Jordan
Sandy
Tooele

Park City Silver Mine Adventure

King's Peak (13,528 ft.)

Uinta R.

Vernal

Timpanogos Cave National Monument

Heber City

N. Fk. Duchesne R.

Roosevelt

Dinosaur National Monument

Orem
Provo

Utah Lake

Strawberry Reservoir

Duchesne

Strawberry R.

White R.

Nephi

Helper
Price

Sevier R.

Sevier Bridge Reservoir

Ephraim

Price R.

Green R.

Willow Cr.

Sevier Lake (dry)

Richfield

Muddy R.

Arches National Park

Colorado R.

Otter Cr.

Fremont R.

Dirty Devil R.

Green R.

Moab

Capitol Reef National Park

Canyonlands National Park

Dixie National Forest

East Fork Sevier R.

Escalante R.

Grand Staircase-Escalante National Monument

Colorado R.

Blanding

Cedar City

Cedar Breaks National Monument

Bryce Canyon National Park

Sevier R.

Lake Powell

San Juan R.

Hovenweep National Monument

Zion National Park

St. George

Frontier Movie Town

BURNING UP THE SALT FLATS

The American Indians, early explorers, and pioneers who shunned the Great Salt Lake Desert would be astonished to see how part of it is used today. Near the town of Wendover, an extremely flat, level area of the desert covering about 30,000 acres (12,141 ha) is known as the Bonneville Salt Flats. Since the early days of automobiles, drivers have found the smooth, hard salt flats an ideal surface for racing. Hundreds of land speed records for cars and motorcycles have been set on the 10-mile (16-km) circular course called the Bonneville Speedway or on straight stretches of the flats themselves. It is one of the few places on Earth with flat, straight, unobstructed courses long enough to allow jet-engine cars to speed up and slow down safely.

Beginning in the 1930s, the speedway began attracting international attention. Such drivers as Sir Malcolm Campbell strove to go faster and faster. British driver John Cobb became the first person to travel on land at more than 400 miles per hour (644 km/h) in 1947. With jet-powered vehicles, the top speeds kept climbing with Craig Breedlove reaching over 600 miles per hour (965 km/h) in 1965. Gary Gabolich topped that in 1970, reaching more than 622 miles per hour (1,001 km/h) in his rocket car.

Once called an "empty, useless wasteland" by a U.S. Army surveyor in the 1850s, the Utah speedway draws drivers and spectators from around the world for its annual Bonneville Nationals Speed Week.

Moving southwest from Moab you'll arrive at Canyonlands National Park. In the area known as Island in the Sky, you can check out the sights from this amazing mesa, which stands more than 1,000 feet (305 m) above the surrounding lands.

As you travel farther south into the Needles district of the park, you'll reach the Confluence Outlook, a peninsula with a dizzying panoramic view of canyons, cliffs, spires, and buttes. Far below, too deep in their canyons to be seen, the Green and Colorado rivers meet. Explorer John Wesley Powell passed this spot in 1869 when he led the first expedition ever to float down the Green and the lower Colorado. No doubt he would be amazed to see the rubber rafts carrying adventurous tourists through those surging waters today.

Heading deeper into the Needles area, you will see what one travel writer described as a "weird sandstone forest" of sharp red-rock pinnacles. You'll find traces of human presence at Cave Spring—battered wooden furniture made and left under a rock overhang by cowboys who herded cattle here in the early twentieth century.

Swing farther south and follow a dirt road to Hovenweep National Monument, the largest set of Ancestral Puebloan (Anasazi) ruins in this part of the Four Corners. Hovenweep was once a thriving community, but now it is precisely what its name means in the Paiute-Ute language: "deserted valley." To

Take a glimpse into the past of the ancestral Puebloan people at Hovenweep National Monument.

the west is another national monument, Natural Bridges. It has three of the world's largest rock bridges (unlike arches, bridges are formed by streams flowing underneath).

Heading west, you must cross Glen Canyon, now filled with the backed-up waters of the Colorado River. There are two ways of crossing, a bridge and a ferry. Both offer dramatic views of cliffs, water, and pleasure boats cruising the Colorado. On the other side of Glen Canyon you'll move toward the third in southern Utah's necklace of national parks, Capitol Reef. Along the way the road passes one of the few human monuments in this vast lonely landscape. A tiny stone cabin at the dusty bottom of a cliff is all that remains of the 1882 homestead of Elijah Behunin, his wife Tabitha, and eleven of their thirteen children. Theirs must have been a hard life—the cabin was so small that the older children slept outside. The Behunin boys slept in a rock alcove in the cliff, and the girls had a wagon box near the cabin for a bedroom.

Capitol Reef gets its name from a huge rock formation that, from some angles, resembles the dome of the Capitol in Washington, D.C. The park lies along a 100-mile (161-km) fold in the earth's surface. Because pools of rainwater sometimes form in bowl-shaped depressions along this steep wrinkle, it is called the Waterpocket Fold. The pools sustain wildlife ranging from spadefoot toads to bighorn sheep and bobcats. A 10-mile (16-km) scenic tour route lets you experience a bit of the park from your car, but it is better to explore it on foot. A restored one-room log schoolhouse in the park is a relic of Fruita, a former Mormon community. After the area was made a national monument in 1937, the people moved away, but the hardy orchards they had planted bear fruit to this day. Capitol Reef became a national park in 1971.

TEN LARGEST CITIES

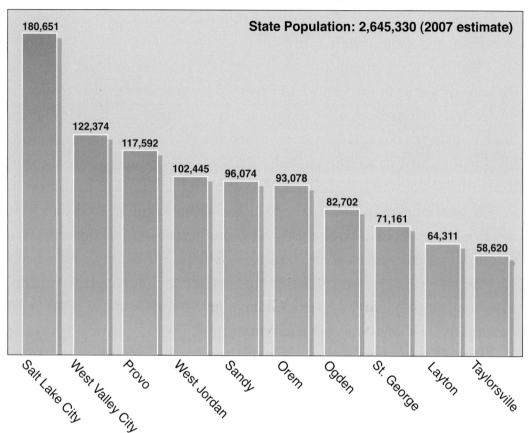

State Population: 2,645,330 (2007 estimate)

Salt Lake City: 180,651
West Valley City: 122,374
Provo: 117,592
West Jordan: 102,445
Sandy: 96,074
Orem: 93,078
Ogden: 82,702
St. George: 71,161
Layton: 64,311
Taylorsville: 58,620

THE SOUTHWEST

West of Capitol Reef you'll enter the High Plateau Mountains on a road that climbs into the Dixie National Forest. The tall trees and green grass are cool and refreshing after so many miles of rock.

Coming down out of the forest, you'll skirt the northern edge of Grand Staircase–Escalante National Monument. A few stunning canyons and arches can be visited by car along the fringe

The Grand Staircase, which encompasses a large area of multicolored cliffs and twisting canyons, is a popular spot for hiking.

of this vast expanse, but real exploration calls for backcountry hiking. Be warned—this monument is not for the inexperienced or unprepared!

On the western edge of Grand Staircase–Escalante lies Utah's fourth nation-al park, Bryce Canyon. It consists of a series of breaks, or semicircular bowls like amphitheaters, that erosion has carved into a 2,000-foot (610-m) pink cliff. Stand on the edge of the cliff and look out and down into the breaks at thousands of pink-and-white hoodoos marching into the distance. Or hike a trail down into the "forests" of hoodoos—and back up again, of course. By sunlight Bryce Canyon is a magnificent wonderland of color. By moonlight it is a mysterious, whimsical maze.

Zion National Park in Utah's southwest corner is the opposite of Bryce. Instead of standing high on a rim looking down into the park, you'll enter a deep, narrow canyon between towering vertical walls and crane your neck to look up at their domed tops. American Indians would not live in the canyon—they found it too dark and ominous when evening

Each year millions of people come to Zion National Park to explore its many natural wonders.

shadows fell. Today Zion is one of the most visited parks in the nation, although relatively few people make the tremendous effort to climb its tougher trails, such as the one leading to Observation Point, which requires hikers to climb 2,148 feet (655 m) up steep cliffs to experience in some wondrous views.

Before leaving southern Utah, stop in at least one more of its engaging towns. You could visit the busy southern city of Saint George, which maintains the first Mormon Temple built in Utah. "Utah's summer spends the winter in Saint George," boast townsfolk, proud of their mild winter weather. Brigham Young must have agreed—he spent his winters in Saint George, where the house he built around 1873 is open to tourists.

Another colorful stop in southern Utah is Kanab, gateway to the North Rim of Arizona's Grand Canyon. So many movie and television Westerns have been filmed around Kanab that locals call the place Little Hollywood.

If you have time for yet one more spectacular sight, and would like a bit more geology, go to Cedar Breaks National Monument, which one ranger calls "Utah's best spot that no one visits." Like Bryce Canyon but smaller and higher, Cedar Breaks is a string of red-rock amphitheaters. With its rim more than 10,000 feet (3,048 m) above sea level, the monument area gets roughly 15 feet (4.5 m) of snow each winter, which can lead to drifts as high as 30 to 40 feet (9 to 12 m) blocking the roads. Crews are not able to clear the way into Cedar Breaks until mid-June some years. Perched between Utah's high country and its western deserts, Cedar Breaks is as wild and beautiful as anything in the state, a good place to say farewell to "the land no one wanted."

THE FLAG: Adopted in 1913, the state flag shows the state seal with a yellow border.

THE SEAL: Utah's seal, which was approved in 1896, shows a bald eagle, representing protection, atop a beehive, representing hard work. The hive is surrounded by sego lilies, which stand for peace. Above the beehive is the word Industry, the state motto; below it are the dates 1847, the year the first Mormons arrived in Utah, and 1896, the year Utah became a state.

State Survey

Statehood: January 4, 1896

Origin of Name: From the Ute Indians, whose name means "people of the mountains"

Nickname: Beehive State

Capital: Salt Lake City

Motto: Industry

Insect: Honeybee

Bird: California gull

Flower: Sego lily

Tree: Blue spruce

Animal: Rocky Mountain elk

Fish: Bonneville cutthroat trout

Gem: Topaz

Grass: Indian rice grass

California gull

Sego lily

UTAH, THIS IS THE PLACE

In 2003 the state legislature decided to change the state song to "Utah, This is the Place." The song was written by Sam and Gary Francis for Utah's centennial celebration in 1996. On behalf of the Cook Elementary School in Syracuse, Representative Dana Love sponsored a bill to make "Utah, This is the Place" the state song because the students enjoyed singing that tune more than the original state song, "Utah, We Love Thee." That musical composition, written by Evan Stephens, had been the official state song since 1937. After "Utah, This is the Place" was made the state song, "Utah, We Love Thee" became the state's official hymn.

Words by Sam Francis and Gary Francis   **Music by Gary Francis**

Fruit: Cherry

Vegetable: Spanish sweet onion

Historic vegetable: Sugar beet

Mineral: Copper

Fossil: Allosaurus

GEOGRAPHY

Highest Point: 13,528 feet (4,123 m) above sea level, at Kings Peak

Lowest Point: 2,350 feet (716 m) above sea level, at Beaver Dam Wash in Washington County

Area: 82,144 square miles (212,752 sq km)

Greatest Distance, North to South: about 347 miles (558 km)

Greatest Distance, East to West: about 272 miles (438 km)

Bordering States: Idaho to the north, Wyoming to the northeast, Colorado to the east, Arizona to the south, Nevada to the west

Hottest Recorded Temperature: 117 °F (47 °C) in Saint George on July 5, 1985

Coldest Recorded Temperature: –69 °F (–56 °C) at Peter's Sink on February 1, 1985

Average Annual Precipitation: 10–15 inches (25–38 cm)

Major Rivers: Bear, Colorado, Green, Provo, San Juan, Sevier, Weber

Major Lakes: Bear, Clear, Great Salt, Powell, Utah

Trees: aspen, balsam, birch, box elder, cottonwood, fir, juniper, maple, mesquite, oak, pine, spruce, willow

Wild Plants: creosote, greasewood, Indian paintbrush, lupine, prickly pear, sagebrush, yucca

Animals: badger, bat, black bear, bobcat, coyote, elk, fox, mountain lion, mule deer, muskrat, rabbit, scorpion, skunk, squirrel

Birds: duck, eagle, goose, grouse, heron, hummingbird, owl, pheasant, quail, seagull, sparrow, swallow, titmouse

Fish: bass, carp, catfish, grayling, perch, trout, whitefish

Endangered Animals: black-footed ferret, bonytail chub, Colorado pikeminnow, humpback chub, June sucker, Kanab ambersnail, razorback sucker, Southwestern willow flycatcher, Virgin River chub, woundfin

Endangered Plants: autumn buttercup, Barneby reed-mustard, Barneby ridge-cress, clay phacelia, dwarf bearclaw-poppy, Holmgren milkvetch, Kodachrome bladderpod, San Rafael cactus, Shivwits or Shem milkvetch, shrubby reed-mustard, Wright fishhook cactus

Southwestern willow flycatcher

TIMELINE

Utah History

c. 500 Ancestral Puebloan arrive in southern Utah.

c. 1300 Fremont and Ancestral Puebloan people disappear from the state.

c. 1500s The Navajo move into present-day southern Utah.

1765 Spaniard Juan Antonio Rivera becomes the first European known to enter Utah.

1776 Silvestre Vélez de Escalante and Francisco Domínguez travel from Santa Fe, New Mexico, to Utah Lake in search of a route to California.

1824–1825 Jim Bridger is one of the first white people to see the Great Salt Lake.

1847 The first Mormons reach Utah.

1848 The United States gains possession of Utah from Mexico.

1850 Utah Territory is established.

1852 Brigham Young, president of the LDS (Mormon) Church, publicly proclaims practice of polygamy.

1856–1860 Three thousand Mormons personally haul their possessions to Utah in what is known as the Handcart Migration.

1857 President James Buchanan sends troops to Utah to enforce his appointment of the territorial governor, resulting in the short-lived Utah War.

1861 Telegraph lines meet in Salt Lake City, connecting the east and west coasts.

1863 U.S. troops killed more than 250 Shoshones in the Bear River Massacre.

1867 The Mormon Tabernacle is completed in Salt Lake City.

1869 The first railroad line across the United States is completed at Promontory Summit.

1890 The leader of the Mormon Church advises Mormons to cease the practice of polygamy.

1896 Utah becomes the forty-fifth state of the Union.

1900 Two hundred people are killed in a mine explosion at Winter Quarters, near Scofield.

1915 Labor leader Joe Hill is convicted of murder and executed, making headlines around the world.

1917–1918 The United States is engaged in World War I.

1940 U.S. Army Air Force opens base at Hill Field.

1942 Topaz, a Japanese civilian internment camp, opens in Utah.

1964 Flaming Gorge Dam is completed, creating Flaming Gorge Reservoir.

1966 Glen Canyon Dam is completed, creating Lake Powell.

1973 Utah Antiquities Act is passed.

1978 The LDS church lifts restrictions against African-American males joining the priesthood.

1996 President Bill Clinton creates the Grand Staircase–Escalante National Monument in western Utah.

2002 Salt Lake City hosts the Winter Olympics.

2007 Utah electorate vote down school vouchers in the state's first referendum since 1974.

ECONOMY

Agricultural Products: apples, apricots, barley, beef cattle, cherries, corn, eggs, greenhouse and nursery plants, hay, hogs, milk, peaches, pears, potatoes, sheep, turkeys, wheat

Manufactured Products: computer and electronic products, food products, medical instruments, newspapers, sporting goods, steel, transportation equipment

Natural Resources: coal, copper, gold, magnesium, natural gas, petroleum, salt, silver, uranium

Business and Trade: banking, engineering, insurance, real estate, tourism, wholesale and retail trade

Apricots

CALENDAR OF CELEBRATIONS

Sundance Film Festival Independent films by young filmmakers are the focus of this world-famous festival held in Park City each January.

Easter Rendezvous at Fort Buenaventura Every Easter weekend in Ogden men and women wearing skins and furs demonstrate their skill at leatherwork, musket shooting, and cooking over a Dutch oven.

Last Spike Ceremony Each May 10 costumed actors at the Golden Spike National Historic Site reenact the driving of the golden spike that completed the first railroad across the United States.

Living Traditions Festival Singers and dancers representing the many ethnic groups that have made Salt Lake City what it is celebrate their collective heritage at this May event.

Scandinavian Heritage Festival Each May, Ephraim revels in its Scandinavian background with lots of traditional food, music, dancing, and crafts.

Northern Ute Fourth of July Pow Wow People from all over the West travel to Fort Duchesne on the Uintah and Ouray Indian

Northern Ute Fourth of July Pow Wow

Reservation each July to enjoy the dance competitions, rodeo, and crafts exhibits.

Days of '47 The first Mormons arrived in the Salt Lake City region in July 1847. Each year, the city celebrates this event with concerts, fireworks, the state's largest rodeo, and one of the nation's largest parades.

Festival of the American West Utah's pioneer past is remembered in Logan during late July and early August with two weeks of mock shootouts, cowboy poetry, square dancing, and panning for gold.

Timpanogos Storytelling Festival Everyone enjoys the spellbinding tales woven by the talented storytellers who gather at Orem for this August event.

Melon Days The tiny town of Green River honors its tasty cantaloupes and watermelons with a September celebration that features a parade, square dancing, and free melons of all kinds.

Greek Festival Lively dancing, cooking demonstrations, delicious food, and even a road race are all part of this September Salt Lake City celebration.

Christmas Village A parade and tree-lighting ceremony in late November kick off Christmastime in Ogden, when the municipal park comes alive with thousands of tiny lights and animated figures.

Days of '47

STATE STARS

Hal Ashby (1936–1988), a film director, was born in Ogden. Ashby first earned acclaim as a film editor, winning an Academy Award in 1967 for *In the Heat of the Night*. He made his directing debut in 1970 with *The Landlord*. Ashby soon developed a reputation for making oddly humorous films, such as *Harold and Maude*, the story of the relationship between a spirited old woman and a teenage boy obsessed with death. He also directed such popular films as *Shampoo*, *Being There*, and *Coming Home*.

Roseanne Barr (1952–   ), an actor and comedian known for her irreverent and sometimes abrasive humor, was born in Salt Lake City. She was a housewife and mother of three when she began doing stand-up comedy in the early 1980s. Her aggressive routines about being a housewife soon earned her national attention. In 1988 she began appearing in her own television show, *Roseanne*, in which she played a feisty working-class mother. She has also appeared in movies, written two books, and hosted her own talk show.

Roseanne Barr

Jim Bridger (1804–1881), one of the most famous mountain men, was one of the first white men to see the Great Salt Lake. Bridger, who was born in Virginia, joined his first fur-trapping expedition in 1822. In the following decades he often served as a guide and scout, so that over his lifetime, he explored much of the West.

John Browning (1855–1926) was perhaps the most successful inventor of firearms in American history. Browning, who began working in his father's gunsmith shop while still a child, made his first gun when he was thirteen years old. His most famous inventions were the Winchester repeating rifle and the Browning automatic rifle, both of which became standard weapons in the U.S. Army. Browning was born in Ogden.

Nolan Bushnell (1943–) invented *Pong*, the world's first video game. In 1972, the same year *Pong* went on the market, he also founded Atari, an early powerhouse in the video game market. Bushnell was born in Ogden and attended the University of Utah.

Nolan Bushnell

Mario Capecchi (1937–) was born in Italy, but has lived in Utah for decades. He is a professor of human genetics at the University of Utah School of Medicine. In 2007 Capecchi shared the Nobel Prize in Physiology or Medicine with other scientists for his work on stem cells and DNA in mammals.

Jack Dempsey (1895–1983) was the
world heavyweight boxing champion
from 1919 to 1926. Dempsey was
born in Colorado and moved to Utah
when he was a child. He first entered
the ring in 1914 and in the next few
years won almost every bout by a
knockout. Dempsey was a powerful,
relentless puncher and often defeated
much larger men. He was elected to
the Boxing Hall of Fame in 1990.

Jack Dempsey

Philo T. Farnsworth (1906–1971), the inventor of television, was born
in Beaver. As a child, Farnsworth loved to tinker with things, and he
won a national invention contest at age thirteen. He came up with the
concept of television while still in high school and by age twenty-one
had produced a working model. Farnsworth also developed the first
simple electron microscope and an early type of radar. In his lifetime,
he had registered three hundred patents, more than one hundred of
them related to television.

John Dennis Fitzgerald (1907–1988), a native of Price, was a beloved
children's author, most famous for his Great Brain series. These
humorous tales concern the adventures of two brothers—one of
them a brilliant schemer—growing up in Utah a hundred years ago.
Fitzgerald also wrote adult books, including the memoir *Papa Married
a Mormon*, about his youth in Utah.

Orrin Hatch (1934–   ) has been a U.S. senator since 1977. Hatch was born in Pennsylvania, attended Brigham Young University, and became a lawyer in Salt Lake City. Although he had never before held elective office, he won election to the U.S. Senate in 1976. Since then, he has established himself as one of the Senate's leading conservative voices.

William D. "Big Bill" Haywood (1869–1928), a native of Salt Lake City, was one of the most famous labor leaders of the early twentieth century. Haywood became a miner at age fifteen and eventually led the Western Federation of Miners. He also helped found the Industrial Workers of the World (IWW), a radical labor organization. In 1918 he was convicted of crimes against the state for opposing U.S. efforts in World War I. To avoid prison, he fled to Russia, which was then the communist nation called the Soviet Union (USSR). He lived there until his death in 1928.

Jon M. Huntsman Sr. (1937–   ) is the chairman and founder of the Huntsman Corporation, an international chemical company. He has spent much of his wealth to help others in need. With his wife, Karen, Huntsman helped establish the Huntsman Cancer Institute in Salt Lake City.

J. Willard Marriott (1900–1985) founded the Marriott Corporation, which runs hundreds of hotels and restaurants. He was born in the town of Marriott, which was named after his grandfather, who had taken part in the 1847 Mormon migration to Utah. While attending the University of Utah, Marriott opened a root-beer stand. In 1927 he decided a root-beer stand would thrive in Washington, D.C., because

Orrin Hatch

of the hot summers, so he started one there. Soon he expanded the menu to include hot food, and the restaurants began multiplying. In 1957 he opened the first Marriott Hotel. Marriott continued as president of the Marriott Corporation until 1964.

Harold Ross (1892–1951) was the founding editor of the prestigious magazine *The New Yorker*. Born in Colorado, he moved to Salt Lake City when he was very young. Ross became interested in journalism in high school, and in 1906 he became an apprentice reporter for the *Salt Lake City Tribune*. He worked for a variety of newspapers before cofounding *The New Yorker* in 1925. The magazine quickly became famous for its wit, sophistication, and excellent writers and cartoonists. Ross himself was renowned for his precise editing and remarkable literary judgment.

Harold Ross

Jedediah Strong Smith (1799–1831) was the first white man to travel the length and breadth of Utah. Smith, a New York native, was a fur trapper and explorer. In 1826 he became the first American to enter California from the east. He also helped open up the coastal trading route from California to Oregon.

Virginia Sorensen (1912–1991), who wrote books for both children and adults, was born in Provo and grew up in Manti. Her works for children include *The House Next Door*, about a teenage girl living in Salt Lake City a century ago, and *Miracles on Maple Hill*, about a city girl who moves to a farmhouse, which earned the Newbery Medal in 1957 for best children's book.

Wallace Stegner (1909–1993) was a leading writer about the West and the environment. Stegner was born in Iowa but moved to Utah as a child. He attended the University of Utah, where he also taught. His writings include *The Gathering of Zion*, a history of the Mormon Trail, and *Angle of Repose*, a Pulitzer Prize–winning novel about a man looking into the lives of his pioneer grandparents. Stegner won the National Book Award in 1977 for his novel *The Spectator Bird*, which concerns the memories of a literary agent.

May Swenson (1919–1989) was a renowned poet noted for her precise imagery. She was born in Logan and attended Utah State University. Her poetry collections include *Another Animal*, *A Cage of Spines*, and *To Mix with Time*. She also wrote three books of poetry for children, including *The Complete Poems to Solve*.

Brigham Young (1801–1877) was the second president of the Jesus Christ of Latter-day Saints Church. Young, who was born in Vermont, converted to Mormonism in 1832. When Joseph Smith, the founder of Mormonism, was killed, Young took over as head of the church. He directed the migration of thousands of Mormons to Utah beginning in 1847. He founded Salt Lake City and oversaw the establishment of hundreds of

Mormon towns. When Utah became a U.S. territory in 1850, he was appointed territorial governor. Although Young ceased being governor after 1857, he remained president of the church until his death.

Loretta Young (1913–2000), a beautiful actress from Salt Lake City, made almost a hundred films in the 1930s and 1940s. Young, who projected a wholesome image, became famous for such films as *Platinum Blonde* and *The Stranger*. In 1947 she won an Academy Award for her performance in *The Farmer's Daughter*, as a Swedish immigrant who starts out a maid and ends up a congresswoman. In the 1950s she had her own television show, *The Loretta Young Show*, for which she won three Emmy Awards.

Loretta Young

Steve Young (1961–   ) is the one of most accurate passers in football history. He began setting records when he was still a quarterback at Brigham Young University. As quarterback for the San Francisco 49ers, he led the National Football League (NFL) in passing four years in a row, a new record. He was named NFL Player of the Year twice and threw a remarkable six touchdowns in the 1995 Super Bowl. Young, a great-great-great-grandson of Brigham Young, was born in Salt Lake City.

TOUR THE STATE

Miles Goodyear Cabin (Ogden) The oldest non-Indian building in Utah, this tiny cabin was built in 1845 from cottonwood logs.

Hill Aerospace Museum (Roy) At this museum, you can get a close-up view of all sorts of military aircraft, including the SR-71 "Blackbird" spy plane.

Hill Aerospace Museum

Antelope Island State Park

Antelope Island State Park (Syracuse) Floating is so easy in the Great Salt Lake, you'll feel like you can walk on water. Antelope Island, which lies 7 miles (11 km) out in the lake, is also a great place for hiking and wildlife viewing—you might even see buffalo!

Mormon Tabernacle (Salt Lake City) This dome-shaped building where the Mormon Tabernacle Choir sings is famed for its amazing acoustics and its gigantic pipe organ, which has close to 12,000 pipes.

Wheeler Historic Farm (Salt Lake City) Tour the farmhouse, milk cows, and take a hayride at this restored farm from the early years of the twentieth century.

Pioneer Memorial Museum (Salt Lake City) This fun museum displays everything from quilts to a mule-drawn streetcar.

Alta Ski Area (Alta) Glide down the slopes at one of the world's best ski areas, famed for its powdery snow.

Heber Valley Railroad (Heber City) Antique trains take visitors into Provo Canyon all the way to Vivian Park, the perfect place for a picnic.

John Hutchings Museum of Natural History (Lehi) You'll see fossils, Indian arts, unusual rocks, and much more in this wide-ranging collection.

Pioneer Memorial Museum

Goblin Valley State Park

Timpanogos Cave National Monument (American Fork) Few caves are as colorful as this one located high in a scenic canyon. It is packed with mineral formations, some of them light shades of green, yellow, and red.

McCurdy Historical Doll Museum (Provo) More than four thousand dolls are exhibited in this unusual museum. They range from Hopi kachinas to figures of presidents.

Goblin Valley State Park (Green River) A favorite pastime among young and old alike in Utah is running and hiding among the oddly shaped formations in this park. Some look like toadstools while others resemble goblins and other scary creatures.

Flaming Gorge National Recreation Area (Dutch John area) Boaters, swimmers, fishers, and water-skiers all love this site. You can also enjoy some gorgeous hikes and check out the Flaming Gorge Dam, where giant turbines and generators transform the flowing water of the Green River into electricity.

Dinosaur National Monument (Jensen) Many of the dinosaur skeletons on display at natural history museums around the country were found at this spot, where you can still watch scientists carefully unearth fossilized dinosaur bones.

Flaming Gorge National Recreation Area

PLEASE
DO NOT
SIT HERE

Dinosaur National Monument

Arches National Park (Moab) On a visit to this park, you'll be surrounded by more than two thousand red sandstone arches, from tiny to towering.

Newspaper Rock (Moab) Come and see fascinating artwork that was scratched into the soft surface of this rock by prehistoric peoples.

Newspaper Rock

Canyonlands National Park (Moab) Check out the fantastic views at Island in the Sky or wander through the red-rock spires of the Needles district at this sprawling park.

Hovenweep National Monument (Bluff) The Ancestral Puebloan people constructed the massive buildings at this monument more than eight hundred years ago. One of the most interesting ruins is Square Tower, which experts believe may have been used as an observatory.

Bryce Canyon National Park (Bryce Canyon) You can explore colorful limestone formations, hike through cool forests, or snowshoe through the silence in the dead of winter at this fantastic national park.

Frontier Movie Town (Kanab) Many Westerns were filmed in Kanab, where you can visit some of the buildings that served as sets and see displays of movie memorabilia.

Coral Pink Sand Dunes State Park (Kanab) You'll feel like you're on another planet when you're in the middle of this vast sea of pink sand.

Zion National Park (Springdale) With its towering cliffs, deep chasms, spectacular hiking trails, and lovely waterfalls, Zion National Park has something to satisfy everyone.

FUN FACTS

The largest natural stone bridge in the world is Utah's Rainbow Bridge National Monument. It soars to a height of 290 feet (88 m) and is 275 feet (84 m) across.

Coral Pink Sand Dunes State Park

When Martha Hughes Cannon was elected to the Utah state senate in 1896, the event made headlines across the nation for two reasons. Not only had she become the country's first female state senator but she had defeated her own husband in the election.

In 1912 voters in Kanab made history when they elected a woman to serve as mayor and four more women to fill all the positions on the town's board, creating the first all-female city government in the nation's history.

FIND OUT MORE

If you'd like to learn more about Utah, look for the titles below in your local library or bookstore. The websites listed at the end offer information and links to other resources.

GENERAL STATE BOOKS

Kent, Deborah. *Utah* (America the Beautiful series). Danbury, CT: Children's Press, 2008.

Sanders, Doug. *Utah* (It's My State Series). Tarrytown, NY: Benchmark Books, 2004.

SPECIAL INTEREST BOOKS

Johnson, Michael and Duncan Clarke. *Native Tribes of the Great Basin and Plateau*. Milwaukee, WI: World Almanac Library, 2004.

Naden, Corrine J. and Rose Blue. *Mormonism*. San Diego, CA: Lucent Books, 2004.

Sonneborn, Liz. *The Mormon Trail*. Danbury, CT: Franklin Watts, 2005.

WEBSITES

History for Kids
http://historyforkids.utah.gov

This site provides information on the state and its rich history just for young people. There's a state timeline, interesting facts, games, links, and even homework help available here.

The Official Utah Government Site
www.utah.gov
This is the place for everything and nearly anything Utah. You can find all of the state agencies here and learn about the latest programs and projects occurring in Utah.

The Utah Travel Industry
www.utah.com
This site offers a treasure of information on places, attractions, and fun activities for those interested in visiting the Beehive State.

Index

Page numbers in **boldface** are illustrations and charts.

ABOUT THE AUTHORS

Rebecca Stefoff is the author of many nonfiction books for young readers, including several other titles on western states in the Celebrate the States series. One of her favorite pastimes is setting out from her home in Portland, Oregon, to explore the back roads and hiking trails of the Pacific Northwest and the Rocky Mountains.

Wendy Mead is a freelance writer and editor. In her work she has tackled a variety of subjects for young readers—from Arizona to alternative music, from birds to biographies. She has visited Utah several times and enjoyed hiking at Zion National Park and at Arches National Park.